# play like

# Eric Clapton

## The Ultimate Guitar Lesson

### by Chad Johnson

To access audio visit:
**www.halleonard.com/mylibrary**

"Enter Code"
"6347-1804-7700-5832"

Cover photo by Rob Verhorst/Redferns/Getty Images

ISBN 978-1-4803-5390-9

# HAL•LEONARD®
## CORPORATION
7777 W. BLUEMOUND RD. P.O.BOX 13819 MILWAUKEE, WI 53213

# CONTENTS

# INTRODUCTION

You hold in your hands the ultimate guide to learning to play like Eric Clapton. Hal Leonard's *Play Like...* series takes a closer look at the styles of guitar giants than any instructional guide before, dissecting every aspect of tone, technique, and magic they impart on the instrument. Eric Clapton has exerted one of the most powerful effects on the guitar world of anyone, and his impact can not be overstated. This book aims to celebrate his accomplishments and help illuminate his methods, preferences, habits, and innovations throughout his illustrious 50-year (and then some) career.

The book is organized into several chapters, each focusing on different aspects of Clapton's complete guitar picture. Here's a quick rundown of what to expect:

## Tale of the Tone

It may very well all be in the fingers, but it's still nice to know what they actually played and when. This section will explore Clapton's gear throughout his career—from his earliest days as a Yardbird to his continued success as a solo artist.

## Songs

In this chapter we'll take a look at transcriptions of five classic songs and examine Clapton's guitar work closely on each one. Each will have an accompanying lesson and other helpful tidbits as well. Each song is demonstrated on the audio with a full band track.

## Essential Licks

This section is all about licks—lots of 'em. They're all in the style of Clapton and all help to illustrate concepts and techniques that Clapton has relied upon throughout his career. Each lick will be demonstrated on the audio.

## Essential Riffs

Though celebrated early on mostly for his leads, Clapton has laid down some killer riffs as well. Here we'll look at ten of the best, again with accompanying lessons and audio.

## Integral Techniques

In this section we'll look at Clapton's technique on the instrument and how it affects his tone, phrasing, and overall approach to the guitar.

## Stylistic DNA

Here we'll look at those hard-to-pinpoint aspects of Clapton's playing that help let us know it's him. Everyone has a different sonic fingerprint on the instrument, and this chapter will help illuminate why Clapton's sounds the way it does.

## Must Hear

Over a career that spans more than half a century, Mr. Clapton has recorded a few bits that you may want to check out. We'll look at the absolute essentials here.

## Must See

Clapton has graced quite a few videos as well, and that's the focus of this chapter. This will also include YouTube videos as well.

# ABOUT THE AUDIO

To access the audio examples that accompany this book, simply go to **www.halleonard.com/mylibrary** and enter the code found on page 1. This will grant you instant access to every example. The examples that include audio are marked with an audio icon throughout the book.

# TALE OF THE TONE

As much as anyone, "Slowhand" has helped define what an electric guitar should sound like in numerous genres, ensembles, and eras. His impact in this regard during the '60s was nothing short of colossal, rivaled only in the world of rock by Hendrix. In this chapter, we'll take an in-depth look at what his tone-shaping tools were and how he wrangled them.

## The Yardbirds

The Yardbirds were the band responsible for first making a name for Clapton, and though his stint with them was brief (1963 to 1965), he experimented with his sound a good deal. Let's examine the key ingredients.

### Guitars

- **Fender Telecaster (red, year unknown)**: This stock Fender guitar belonged to the band and was also used by Jeff Beck during his time with the Yardbirds before he purchased his Fender Esquire.

- **Gretsch Chet Atkins Tennessean (red, 1958)**: Clapton used this guitar only briefly during his Yardbird years, stating that it didn't fit his kind of sound. It featured a mahogany neck, ebony fretboard, and Bigsby vibrato. It was eventually sold at an auction to benefit the Crossroads Centre, a treatment center in Antigua for substance abuse.

- **Gibson ES-335 (cherry red, 1964)**: This is one of Clapton's most famous guitars and, along with the Telecaster, his most-used guitar while in the Yardbirds. He played this guitar through his time with the Bluesbreakers, Cream, Blind Faith, and much of his solo career. It eventually sold for nearly $850,000 at auction in 2004.

- **Gibson Les Paul (cherry sunburst, 1960)**: Clapton bought this guitar toward the end of his stint with the Yardbirds, so it didn't get used much in that band. It went on to become his main guitar with the Bluesbreakers. It featured two PAF pickups and a slim profile neck.

- **Fender Jazzmaster (sunburst, year unknown)**: Clapton can be seen in various photos from live shows with the Yardbirds playing a sunburst Jazzmaster, though its use other than that is little-documented.

### Amps

- **Vox AC30**: This was Clapton's main (and most likely only) amp used during the Yardbirds years. This was a very common choice for the British bands of the day.

## The Bluesbreakers

After the Yardbirds released the pop song "For Your Love," Clapton threw in the towel in protest. Seeking to quench his thirst for more traditional blues with newly acquired Gibson Les Paul in hand, he joined John Mayall's Bluesbreakers only months after leaving the Yardbirds.

### Guitars

- **Gibson Les Paul (cherry sunburst, 1960)**: This was Clapton's main guitar with the band and is featured on the "Beano" album, *Bluesbreakers with Eric Clapton*.

- **Gibson ES-335 (cherry red, 1964)**: Clapton made occasional use of this guitar for live shows with the band.

### Amps

- **Marshall JTM 45 and Marshall 4x12 cabinet**: During his early period with the band, there are photos of him making use of at least two different Marshall half stacks—a badge-logo head and a white-front head—though the exact date is not known.

- **Marshall Series II 1962 Combo**: Jim Marshall has said in the past that it was Clapton who'd been most responsible for the development of the Marshall combo line. Eric wanted an amp that could fit in his truck yet still deliver a fat tone with increased sustain. The Series II 1962 was very similar to a combo version of a JTM 45, but with about 35 watts of power, KT66 output tubes, and a GZ34 rectifier tube (as well as a few other minor circuitry changes). It featured two 12-inch Greenback Celestion G12M speakers. It's this amp that Clapton used on the "Beano" album, and Mike Vernon (producer) is credited with allowing Clapton to break convention and record with the amp turned up as loud as possible in the studio, which was essential in achieving his groundbreaking tone.

## Effects

- **Dallas Rangemaster treble booster**: Though there is very little photo evidence, if any, to support it, it's a common myth that Clapton made use of this unit for the "Beano" album. This "pedal" wasn't really a pedal, because it didn't even feature a footswitch. If you ran through it, it was always on. It had one knob that set the amount of treble boost and that was it. Until it's heard from the horse's mouth—and considering it's going on nearly fifty years since the recording, even the horse may not remember clearly—this myth will most likely continue to circulate and generate debate.

# Cream

If the Bluesbreakers catapulted Clapton to Guitar God status in England, Cream lifted him to the upper echelons of world guitar domination. Clapton, Jack Bruce, and Ginger Baker began rehearsals in mid-1966, and Eric's sound got even louder at this period to compete with the drumming styles of Baker. It's during this era that many fans feel he achieved his most stunning guitar tones of all.

## Guitars

- **Gibson Les Paul (cherry sunburst, 1960)**: He began rehearsing with the same Les Paul he'd used in the Bluesbreakers, but unfortunately the guitar was stolen shortly after in the summer of 1966.

- **Gibson Les Paul (borrowed, vintage sunburst, possibly 1959)**: Though it's unknown as to whom this guitar actually belonged, Clapton was forced to use it on Cream's first album, *Fresh Cream*, which was released in December of 1966. The guitar featured PAF pickups, but with the covers still on (as opposed to his Bluesbreakers guitar, on which they'd been removed), and a Bigsby vibrato.

- **Gibson Les Paul (cherry sunburst, probably 1960)**: Clapton originally borrowed this guitar from Andy Summers, eventually talking Andy into selling it to him. It featured black PAF pickups with the covers removed, a stop tailpiece, and a missing switch plate. It's possible that this guitar was also used on *Fresh Cream*.

- **Gibson ES-335 (cherry red, 1964)**: Eric made good use of this guitar throughout the mid-to-latter part of his time with Cream, especially during live shows. Even though Clapton himself has said it was this one, there is great debate over whether it was this guitar or "The Fool" (see below) on the famous live recording of "Crossroads" from the *Wheels of Fire* album (1968).

- **"The Fool" Gibson SG (custom painted, 1964)**: This is one of Clapton's most famous guitars of all and the instrument most often associated with the "Summer of Love" (1967). Custom-painted by a Dutch artistic duo named "the Fool," it featured "Patent Number Pickups," which followed the PAF ("patent applied for") pickups once the patent had been granted. The guitar appears on the *Disraeli Gears*, *Wheels of Fire*, and *Goodbye* albums and is certainly one his most frequently used guitars from the Cream years. After Clapton gave the guitar to George Harrison, it exchanged hands several more times before being sold to a collector at auction in 2000. Clapton achieved his famous "Woman Tone" on "Sunshine of Your Love" with this guitar, rolling the tone knob nearly all the way off and cranking everything on the Marshall amp to 10.

- **Gibson Reverse Firebird 1 (sunburst, 1964–65)**: Clapton made use of this guitar extensively during live shows beginning in mid-1968. It had one mini-humbucker, volume and tone knobs, a rosewood fretboard, and dot inlays. It is not thought to be featured on any studio Cream recordings, though it appears on some live ones.

- **Gibson Les Paul Custom (black, 1958–59)**: This was a three-pickup model Les Paul that Clapton most likely purchased in the U.S. while on tour in April of 1967. It was used often for live shows and also on *Disraeli Gears*. He continued to play this guitar into his time with Blind Faith (and Delaney and Bonnie).

- **"Lucy" Gibson Les Paul (red, 1957)**: Clapton played this guitar for his famous solo on the Beatles' "While My Guitar Gently Weeps," after which he gave it to George Harrison, who named it "Lucy." It belonged to Rick Derringer before Clapton.

## Amps

- **Marshall JTM100 Model 1959 (100 watts, 1966)**: This is the amp of the early Cream period and was paired with two 4x12 cabinets with 20- or 25-watt speakers. The amp featured KT66 tubes and can be heard on *Fresh Cream* and *Disraeli Gears*. Clapton always plugged into the "Normal" channel on his amps, as opposed to the more popular "Brilliant" channel favored by Hendrix, among others. In the latter part of 1967, after returning from their first major U.S. tour, Clapton switched to two full stacks. He would occasionally use both, either plugging into both with a "Y" cord or using a jumper cord to link them, but he's stated in interviews that the second one was usually just there as a backup.

- **Fender Twin Reverb (blackface)**: There are also pictures of the *Disraeli Gears* sessions showing Fender Twin Reverbs, though it's not known for sure on which songs they were used, if at all.

## Effects

- **Vox V846 Wah (1967)**: Inspired by Hendrix, Clapton added an early version of the Vox wah to his rig in 1967 while working on the *Disraeli Gears* album. It's prominently featured on "Tales of Brave Ulysses" and of course later on "White Room" from *Wheels of Fire*. He also made extensive use of the pedal during live shows from the period.

- **Fender Leslie speaker cabinet**: This was used on the song "Badge" from *Goodbye*, though it most likely belonged to the studio.

# *Blind Faith*

After Cream imploded in 1968, Clapton tried to give the supergroup one more go, recruiting Cream's drummer Ginger Baker and joining English legend Steve Winwood (vocals, guitars, keys) and Ric Grech (bass) to form Blind Faith. They lasted through one eponymous album and one tour—not even a year—before breaking up.

## Guitars

- **Fender Telecaster Custom (sunburst, 1962)**: This was one of Clapton's main guitars during the Blind Faith period. It featured a Strat neck from "Brownie" (see below). It wasn't seen after the band broke up, and its whereabouts are not known.

- **Gibson ES-335 (cherry red, 1964)**: This guitar, along with his Tele Custom, was most likely used on the *Blind Faith* album, as Clapton can be seen with this guitar in the album sleeve.

- **Gibson Reverse Firebird 1 (sunburst, 1964–65)**: Though this guitar may have been featured on the *Blind Faith* album as well, it showed up on a good number of live performances.

## Amps

- **Marshall JTM100 Model 1959 (100 watts, 1966)**: These amps were held over from the Cream days and used presumably both in the studio as well as on stage.

- **Fender Dual Showman Reverb (silverface)**: This is the other amp Clapton used during his Blind Faith tenure, which was also seen both in studio and on stage. It was also a 100-watt amp but featured 6L6GC tubes and a solid state rectifier.

## Effects

- **Vox V846 Wah (1967)**: This is the same wah from the Cream period.

- **Fender Leslie speaker cabinet**: This is the same as used on "Badge."

# *Derek and the Dominos*

Another short-lived phase of Eric's early '70s period, Derek and the Dominos were formed in 1970 by Clapton with most of the members from Delaney, Bonnie & Friends, the group with which Eric had been touring after Blind Faith. They recorded only one studio album, the famous *Layla and Other Assorted Love Songs*, the sessions of which were augmented famously by slide guitar virtuoso Duane Allman.

Though Clapton had been using Fender Stratocasters while on tour with Delaney, Bonnie & Friends, the *Layla...* album marks the first time on record where the basis of his sound had clearly shifted to the Strat. It also marks the beginning of Eric's focus as a singer/songwriter, as opposed to just a guitar virtuoso who occasionally sang some songs. This was largely due to the influence and encouragement of Delaney Bramlett and Bobby Whitlock.

## Guitars

- **"Brownie" Fender Stratocaster (sunburst, 1956)**: Though Clapton bought this guitar in 1967 just before the recording of *Disraeli Gears*, it doesn't appear to have been used on record until *Layla*. Its neck had been transferred to a Tele for his stint in Blind Faith, but it was transferred back for use on this album. Clapton preferred worn necks to new ones in general. This guitar served as a backup once he acquired "Blackie" (see below). Eventually, "Brownie" was sold at auction in 1999 for $497,500 to benefit the Crossroads Centre. It was the most expensive guitar ever sold at the time.

- **Martin or Guild Acoustic**: Eric also played acoustic on the *Layla* album, but little information is known about the make, and it could have very likely been borrowed from the studio.

## Amps

- **Fender Champ**: This is another topic of endless debate. For years, rumors have circulated that Clapton used nothing but a tweed Fender Champ for the entire *Layla* album, and Howard Albert, one of the engineers for the sessions, has stated the same in interviews. However, Tom Dowd, who produced the record, has stated that they were brand new Fender Champs at the time, which would have made them silverface models. He's also stated in an interview though, that Clapton brought a tweed Champ and a Princeton and that Duane Allman played through an old Gibson combo amp—most likely a GA20, GA30, or GA40.

- **Fender Dual Showman Reverb (silverface)**: Clapton used Dual Showmans for some live shows with the Dominos, but they did not show up on the *Layla* album.

- **Marshall JTM100**: He can be seen in some photos with Marshalls as well as on stage.

## Effects

- **Fender Leslie speaker cabinet**: This was modified by the engineers with a Variac, which enabled the control of the rotation speed.

- **Vox V846 Wah (1967)**: The same from his Cream years, you can hear this all over the *Live at the Fillmore* album.

# Solo Career

With four decades under his belt (and still counting) as a solo artist, Clapton's accumulated gear since the early '70s has, needless to say, been immense. Therefore, the information given here will touch upon the highlights, as anything more would not fit within the scope of this book. Also, guitars and amps that have already been mentioned, such as the famous cherry red Gibson ES-335, which was used on 1989's *Journeyman* and 1994's *From the Cradle*, or "Brownie," which mostly served as a backup guitar to "Blackie," will not be repeated in this list to conserve space.

## Guitars

- **"Blackie" Fender Stratocaster (composite guitar built from 1956 and 1957 parts)**: This guitar was Clapton's #1 instrument from the early '70s through the mid-'80s when it was finally retired due to neck issues. It was assembled from three different mid-'50s Strats that he bought in 1970 at a Tennessee guitar shop (he actually bought six at the time, but he gave one to George Harrison, Pete Townshend, and Steve Winwood). This guitar was also sold at auction in 2004 (to Guitar Center), where it fetched the highest amount ever at the time (surpassing the record held by "Brownie" prior) at $959,500 to benefit the Crossroads Centre.

- **Eric Clapton Fender Stratocasters**: After "Blackie" was retired, Clapton began working with the Fender Custom Shop on the idea of releasing a signature model. Though he began playing prototypes on stage as early as 1986, the first commercially released signature model arrived in 1988—the first signature model ever for Fender. It featured an alder Fender Elite body, Gold Lace Sensor pickups, a V-shaped maple neck, and a mid-boost circuit that helped achieve a more overdriven sound. The guitar has gone through numerous changes over the years, including the replacement of Lace Sensor pickups with Vintage Noiseless ones, and Clapton has made use of many incarnations throughout his career.

- **Gibson Byrdland (several models)**: Clapton has made occasional use of Gibson Byrdlands on stage throughout his career, most notably at the Concert for Bangladesh in 1971 (although there is some debate on this, as the guitar appears to be modified with regards to the fretboard inlays and pickguard). One of his Byrdlands, a 1957 model, fetched $43,000 at an auction to benefit the Crossroads Centre in 1999.

- **Eric Clapton 1960 Gibson Les Paul**: In late 2010, Gibson began collaborating with Clapton on recreating his Bluesbreakers-era Les Paul that was stolen in 1966. This guitar was the result, and Clapton has made occasional use of it on stage.

- **Martin 000-42 Acoustic (1939)**: This is the main guitar Clapton played on the *Unplugged* show. It was this performance that was the genesis for the Clapton signature line of Martins. Featuring Brazilian rosewood back and sides with a spruce top, this guitar went on to sell at auction in 2004 for $791,500, setting another record for the highest-priced acoustic guitar.

- **Martin 000-28 Acoustic (1966)**: This is the other *Unplugged* guitar, which Clapton used less.

- **Eric Clapton Martin Signature Models**: After the *Unplugged* show, Martin was overloaded with requests for information on Clapton's guitar. It was then that Martin approached Eric with the idea for this guitar. First appearing in 1995 as the 000-42EC, it's since spawned several more instruments bearing the Clapton signature. Since Martin guessed that they would sell approximately 500 guitars, they released a limited run of 461 as a nod to Clapton's *461 Ocean Boulevard* album from 1974. First debuted at the Winter NAMM show in 1995, the guitars all sold out in one day. Martin's director of Artists and Public Relations, Dick Boak, has commented that Eric Clapton single-handedly revitalized the life of the small-body Martins.

## Amps

Clapton has experimented a bit more with regards to amps since he fell in love with the Strat. Let's take a look at the most commonly used ones here. Clapton fans are often divided on the topic of Gibson vs. Fender, and the same could be said with regard to his amp choices.

- **Pignose portable amp (1974)**: Eric's been rumored to make use of this little amp in the studio for years and said himself in interviews that he recorded the song "Motherless Children," from *461 Ocean Boulevard*, with nothing but a Pignose amp. This amp sold at auction for $9,760 in 2011.

- **Music Man HD 130 Reverb (130 watts)**: Clapton began using these amps in the mid-'70s with open-back 2x12 cabinets loaded with JBL speakers. They featured master volume controls, which he liked because it allowed him to get the overdriven tone without the searing volume of a cranked Marshall stack. Clapton endorsed Music Man from 1974 to 1983 and can be seen in many magazine ads from this time period.

- **Marshall JCM800 1959 (100 watts) and 1987 (50 watts)**: Around 1984, Clapton switched back from Music Man to newer Marshall amps of the day: the JCM800 in 100 watt (1959 model) and 50 watt (1987 model) configurations. These were master volume amps, similar to the Music Man ones, which enabled a distorted sound at lower volumes. Clapton used these extensively from 1984 to 1987 and on occasion since then.

- **Soldano SLO-100 (100 watts)**: Clapton ordered some custom amps from Soldano after hearing Mark Knopfler's in 1988. The amp featured channel-switching, 5881 output tubes, and an effects loop. He made extensive use of this rig, coupled with the custom-designed effects rig by Pete Cornish (see below), from 1989 to 1993 and could be seen prominently on the *Journeyman* tour and heard on *24 Nights* (1991) and *From the Cradle* (1994).

- **Fender Twin (tweed, 1958)**: Clapton purchased a 1958 tweed twin in the early '80s and had used it in the studio throughout the years. When the amp began to give out, he approached Fender about creating a clone of it. John Suhr, an amp tech at Fender at the time, ended up building three replicas in 1997, and Clapton gave one to B.B. King as a gift. John Suhr went on to found Suhr guitars shortly afterward and eventually added amps to his product line as well.

- **Fender Custom Vibro-King (60 watts)**: Clapton began using these amps during his *Reptile* tour in 2001. The amps feature an unusual 3x10 speaker configuration and were reportedly modified by Fender specifically for Clapton.

- **Cornell Custom 80 (tweed Fender Twin clone)**: After being approached by Clapton's guitar tech in hopes of modifying his Vibro-King amps, Dennis Cornell ended up building Clapton a custom amp, which Eric played at the Queen's Golden Jubilee show in 2002.

- **Fender EC Series Amplifiers (2011)**: Clapton collaborated with Fender in 2011, with three new amps as a result: the EC Twinolux, EC Tremolux, and EC Vibro-Champ. Each one is custom-designed with features requested by Clapton that make them unique from other Fender amps. The Vibro-Champ is based on the tweed Champ, is roughly 5 watts, and features a 6V6 output tube. The Tremolux is based on the tweed Deluxe, outputs about 12 watts, and features two 6V6 output tubes. And the Twinolux is based on the tweed Twin, outputs about 40 watts, and features two 6L6GE output tubes. All three amps feature tremolo. Eric has been seen playing these on stage often, as has Buddy Guy.

## Effects

- **Dunlop Crybaby wah pedal**: At some point in the mid-'70s, Clapton began using a Dunlop Crybaby wah and has, for the most part, continued to favor it over the Vox to this day.

- **Bradshaw Rig**: For the *Behind the Sun* tour in 1985, Clapton began using an effects rack system designed by Bob Bradshaw (a busy man in the '80s!) in order to help recreate the glossy sound he'd achieved in the studio. Among other things, it included an Ibanez HD1000 Harmonics delay, a DBX 160 compressor, a Dyno-My-Piano Tri Stereo Chorus, a Roland SDE-3000 delay, a Boss CE-1 chorus, and a Boss Heavy Metal pedal.

- **Pete Cornish Rig**: For the *Journeyman* tour in 1989, Clapton updated his rig with a new effects system designed by Pete Cornish. It featured a Drawmer Tube Compressor, the Roland SDE-3000, a TC Electronic Spatial Expander, a Yamaha SPX90, the Dyno-My-Piano Tri Stereo Chorus, a TC Electronic 2290 delay, a Dynachord CLS-222 (Leslie simulator), and a Yamaha GEP50.

# SONGS

In this chapter, we're going to look at five complete song transcriptions with a lesson on each. We'll study them in-depth and get specific with any and all techniques needed to play them. By the end of each lesson, you should know everything you need to play the song. Several different eras are covered with regards to the song choices, but it's simply not possible to represent the entire breadth of Clapton's career with five selections. However, suffice it to say that the lion's share of Clapton's continuous guitar legacy is represented in one way or another here.

## Hide Away
### From *Bluesbreakers with Eric Clapton*, 1966

Freddie King, a.k.a. "the Texas Cannonball," first penned and recorded "Hide Away" in 1960 on the Federal label. The song experienced unprecedented crossover success, reaching #5 on the R&B charts and #29 on the pop charts, and it soon became his life-long signature song. A spirited blues shuffle in the guitar lover's key of E, it's been covered by practically everyone and their mother in the blues genre, but the version by John Mayall's Bluesbreakers with Eric Clapton in 1966 certainly stands out as a definitive version all its own.

There are several key differences in the Bluesbreaker version, but the band clearly struck a healthy balance between deference to the original and creative liberty. First of all, they sped up the tempo slightly, which helped support one of the other key traits: the guitar tone. Clapton's high studio volume during the Bluesbreaker sessions was unprecedented at the time, and the resulting tone was thick, distorted, and in your face. It's only natural that the tempo would creep up in the presence of such intensity of sound. In fact, Clapton's Marshall amp had to face the wall and be surrounded by numerous baffles in order to tame the volume enough so that his guitar wouldn't completely bleed over all the other instruments.

You'll also notice that Clapton plays much of the main theme in a different position than King did, which contributes greatly to the thicker tone. Another difference is that Clapton improvised more in general on the track, only stating the main theme once at the beginning before launching into a full-fledged solo, whereas King only slightly embellished the main theme the second time through. For the most part, Clapton neatly organized his solo choruses (one time through a 12-bar form is known as a "chorus") into certain fretboard positions, and we'll take a look at those more closely as we progress.

Let's take a look at the song section by section (using rehearsal letters) and break it down into nicely digestible chunks. For reference, the song transcription begins on page 17.

### Section A – Main Theme

Whereas King stated the main theme of "Hide Away" in open position, Clapton begins in ninth position, playing out of the E major pentatonic scale. This scale form looks like this:

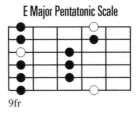

You may recognize this scale form as the C♯ minor pentatonic scale, and you'd be right. C♯ minor is the *relative minor* of E major. That is to say they share the same notes. It's just that, when thinking of this as an E major pentatonic scale, the E note is the tonic—i.e., feels resolved—as opposed to the C♯ minor pentatonic, which treats the C♯ note as the tonic. You'll notice that the E notes in the grid are represented with open circles, indicating that E is the tonic of this scale.

The notation at the beginning of the music that shows two eighth notes equaling a quarter and eighth with a triplet bracket above is simply a way of letting us know that the song is played with a shuffle feel. This means that when eighth notes are seen in the music, they should be played with a lopsided feel—i.e., the first note of each beat will last longer than the second. It's much easier to hear a shuffle than to explain it, so just take a listen to the audio and it will become clear. Everyone has heard a shuffle feel before, and it will be immediately recognizable.

For the pickup phrase, begin in ninth position—meaning that your index finger is on fret 9—and, after the first B note on string 4, partially barre your first finger to cover strings 4 and 3 at fret 9 to play the B/E double stop. Pluck the two notes and then hammer on to fret 11 on string 4 with your ring finger. In all honesty, the double stop may have not been intentional, since he doesn't do this on the repetitions of this same idea, but it sounds nice and thick all the same and makes for a cool intro. Continue to the 9th fret with your index finger, and the pickup phrase is complete.

The official downbeat on measure 1 marks the entrance of the band and kicks off with a whole-step bend on fret 11 of string 3. Although Clapton bends with an unsupported ring finger, this is certainly not the norm, so it's recommended that you use your middle finger behind your ring finger when bending (see photo). Consequently, this same approach would apply to any bending finger: middle, ring, or pinky. The only time you wouldn't support your bending finger is when bending with your index finger, in which case it's not possible.

In measure 2, this original phrase is extended in a somewhat symmetrical fashion, almost forming a musical palindrome of sorts. After ascending up to the bent 11th fret just as in the intro (the only difference being the lack of the double stop), Clapton uses a nifty little trick to dress up the phrase. Instead of just playing the 11th fret on string 3, he first plucks it while it's still bent from beat 3 and then immediately releases the bend as a grace note. It may take a little practice to get this perfectly smooth because it's not a terribly common move, but it's not particularly difficult either.

At measure 3, we land back at the 9th-fret E note on string 3 and apply some healthy vibrato. See the Techniques chapter for more on Clapton's brand of vibrato. On beat 2, the F♯ note at fret 11, string 3 is just hinted at, which serves simply as a little decoration to the main melody note (E). Next comes the fun part: the repetitive triplet hammer-on lick. This isn't a difficult lick, but be sure to keep the notes steady and in tempo. To help practice this, try moving the same idea to different string groups, like this:

Hide Away
Example 1

Measure 6 is essentially a repeat of measure 2, just without the grace-note bend release on fret 11. At the end of measure 7, we see a classic move especially common when being backed up only by a bassist and drummer: a "chord punch." This is a way to suggest some harmony in between your lead lines. Play the 7th fret on string 5 with your middle finger , slide up a half step (one fret), and then add your index and ring fingers on strings 4 and 3, respectively, to form the F7 chord. After picking it, slide back down a half step to the E7 chord without picking.

Interestingly, beginning with the pickup to measure 9, Clapton moves down to open position and finishes out the theme there, Freddie King-style. Most players, including Clapton, use their middle finger for all the fretted notes through the end of measure 10, including the slide up to fret 4. Hammering on from an open string feels a little different than hammering from a fretted note, since you don't already have a finger on the neck to keep it steady, so take it slowly at first and make sure you're being accurate. Try this exercise first and make sure you're only making contact with one string during the hammer-on:

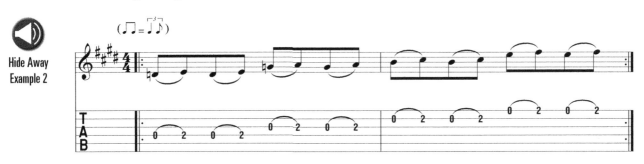

Hide Away
Example 2

Measure 11 opens with a blues guitar staple: the *trill*. The concept is pretty simple; you pluck the open G string and then hammer to fret 1 and pull-off to the open string over and over as fast as possible. It's a bit easier said than done, though, so don't be alarmed if your trills don't sound like Eric's right away. The rest of measure 11 continues with a fairly common turnaround idea in E. Be sure to slightly bend fret 3 on string 2 for a little blues attitude. You'll need to keep your fret-hand finger arched (most likely your middle finger) on beat 3 to allow the open first and second strings to ring along with the fourth fret on string 3. If you're a hybrid picker at all—i.e., the use of pick and fingers to pluck the strings—the beginning of measure 12 would be a prime time to use the technique, as there's quite a bit of string skipping going on.

The second chorus kicks off Clapton's first solo, which is fairly low key, comparatively speaking. For most of this solo, Clapton is working out of the open-position E minor pentatonic scale with a few additions here and there. Here's what this looks like. A few optional notes are shown in grey, which Clapton alludes to occasionally.

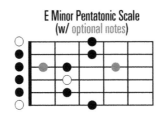

**E Minor Pentatonic Scale**
**(w/ optional notes)**

Right out of the gate, we see another trill on string 3. This one is a bit harder, though, because it's not alone. You'll also need to fret the E note on string 4 while performing the trill on string 3. Lucky for you, it only lasts a quarter note! The dyad of B/D on strings 3 and 2 over the next 2-1/2 measures is a must-know blues guitar move, and Clapton milks it nicely by alternating the B note with the B/D dyad in triplets, which creates a syncopated feel that he rides for two full measures.

In measure 18, Clapton rakes into the E note on string 2. A *rake* is a quick brush through the strings en route to a target note. Rakes are normally ascending, as is this one, though they can be descending as well. The strings being raked can either be actual pitches like these, palm-muted notes, or completely deadened strings that just produce a percussive "pfft" sound. Rakes such as this one are grace notes, meaning they take up no real metric time. It's no coincidence that Clapton is raking through the notes of an A triad here (A–C♯) en route to the E note, since he's playing over A7 at the time. In measure 19, you'll need to silently *pre-bend* fret 7 on string 2 a half step, pick it, and then bend it another half step. This is a tricky move, so check your pitch against unbent notes to make sure you're getting it right.

The triplet figure in measures 20–22 is kind of a thinned out version of measures 14–15 and helps gain some momentum leading into the turnaround. On beat 3 of measure 23, you'll need to pick the 4th-fret note on string 3, fretted with your middle finger, quickly slide down to fret 2, and then pull off to the open G string all in one continuous action. To make sure all the notes are speaking clearly, try this exercise first. Play it slowly and gradually speed it up.

Hide Away
Example 3

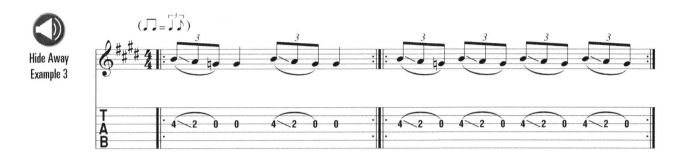

## Section B – Ensemble Riff

At section B, everyone joins in for an ensemble riff that's reminiscent of a piano boogie woogie bass line. Notice that the same riff is essentially transposed for each chord in the section—the only difference being the final note of each phrase, which is always E.

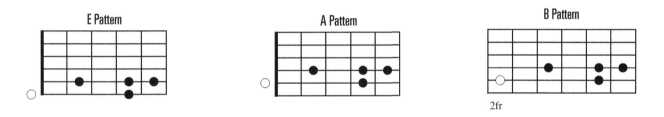

E Pattern                                   A Pattern                                   B Pattern

                                                                                        2fr

Take note of the various slides that Clapton interjects throughout to help bring this riff to life. This type of subtlety can really help keep things fresh, especially when a phrase is being directly transposed like this.

## Section C – Guitar Solo

For the solo proper, Clapton works exclusively out of the 12th position—mostly using the E minor pentatonic scale again. Here's how that looks. I've added an additional note in grey that Clapton adds sporadically. This C♯ note technically comes from the E Dorian mode, but it's a common addition to the minor pentatonic.

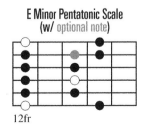

E Minor Pentatonic Scale
(w/ optional note)

12fr

Clapton removes his kid gloves here and knocks down the door right away with a gnarly *unison bend*. Start with your index finger on the 12th fret of string 2 and your ring finger on the 14th fret of string 3. Pick both strings and then bend the note on string 3 up a whole step to match the one on string 2 (see photo). The thing about unison bends is that they're kind of like violins: they can sound really great when they're played well, but they can sound really ugly when they're not. As the pitches get close to matching, you'll hear the same "beats" you hear when you're tuning your strings with your tuning pegs. The closer you get, the slower the beats get, until they eventually stop altogether, which is where you want to be. This particular unison bend goes by very quickly, but there are many times when one is held out for a whole note or longer. In those cases, you really need to have the intonation down.

Clapton continues his bending shenanigans, and by measure 41, we see another must-know bending move: the *double-stop bend*. While fretting the 14th fret on string 3 with the ring finger, he flattens it out to grab string 2 as well, in essence forming a partial barre. He then bends both strings at once up a half step. If you've never done this before, it can feel really strange at first. The alternative is to use the ring finger on string 3 and your pinky on string 2. You'll really need to try both methods out and see what feels better. Some players even switch between the methods depending on the particular lick.

Throughout measures 41–43, you'll get plenty of practice with this concept, and you'll also need to perform double-stop bends on fret 12 with your first finger. (Almost all players would perform these with their first finger only for both notes.) Note, however, that it's customary for this move to be performed by pulling *down* on the strings toward the floor.

Clapton finishes out this solo with an impressive display of minor pentatonic licks that lock steadily into the groove. Save for the G♯ notes in measures 47 and 48, all of these notes come from E minor pentatonic.

## Section D – Stop Time, 6th Riff & Solo

For section D, we have what's called a *stop time* break. This means that the rhythm section hits a chord (usually on the downbeat) and then rests for a measure (or possibly two), allowing the soloist to bask completely in the spotlight. Clapton follows Freddie King's trail here and strums a nice E9 chord in triplets. On beat 3 of measures 49 and 50, he adds a deliberate, descending slide for dramatic effect. Though he's playing only the top three strings here, the chord form is actually this:

E9 Chord

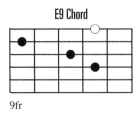

9fr

In measure 51, we get the payoff lick. This is most likely Freddie King's most memorable guitar moment and certainly one of the great licks of the genre. Using a major 6th interval played on strings 1 and 3, Clapton descends down a composite melody that's quite unique. If you look at just the notes on string 1, they form an E major pentatonic scale. But the notes on string 3, which all run parallel with the ones on string 1, form a G major pentatonic scale. G major is the relative major of E minor, so you could also call this an E minor pentatonic scale. So, in essence, you have an E major pentatonic scale harmonizing with an E minor pentatonic scale! Since you never hear a major 3rd and minor 3rd at the same time, the effect is not jarring or displeasing at all. In fact, it's quite a nice, unique sound. (Interestingly, on the original version, Freddie plays G♯ at fret 13 on string 3 at the beginning of the lick instead of G. He then shifts to the parallel fingering and remains throughout the rest of the lick.)

Technically speaking, this riff can be a little tricky. Regarding the fret hand, most players will use the middle finger on string 3 and the ring on string 1. Others may use the ring on string 3 and the pinky on string 1. Clapton uses the former, but try both to see which feels better.

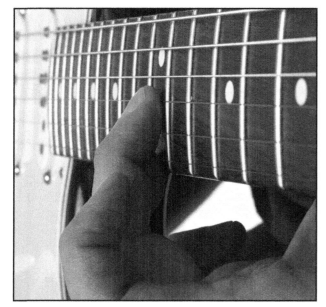

You have two options for picking these 6ths: with the pick, or with hybrid picking (pick and finger together). If you use only the pick, you have the issue of the B string in the middle. You don't want it ringing out, so you'll need to allow either or both fretting fingers to lean against it to deaden it (see photo). That way, you can strum through the top three strings while only hearing strings 3 and 1. If you choose to use hybrid picking, you'll pick the notes on string 3 with a downstroke using the pick and the ones on string 1 with either your second or third finger.

Realize, however, that twice in the lick, you have to pick the open G and open high E strings together, and this can really only be done with hybrid picking. (Freddie King played fingerstyle entirely, so this wasn't an issue for him.) On the Bluesbreakers recording, it sounds as though Clapton uses hybrid picking. However, in some live versions since then, he clearly starts off strumming through the 6ths with the pick. So you'll have to decide for yourself which feels and sounds best.

In measures 54–57, Clapton follows with some tasty licks from the "B.B. King box" in fifth position. This is a composite scale form that only covers the top three strings. It would usually look like this in the key of E:

**B.B. King Box in E**

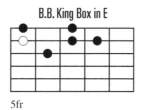

5fr

There's some fancy fretwork here, so go through it slowly. Notice how in measure 55 he bends the 7th fret on string 2 first up a whole step and then continues on up to 1-1/2 steps before coming back down to a whole step. This type of bending control takes practice, not to mention a decent amount of finger strength, so work it up gradually. In measures 58–59, Clapton moves up to another position of the E minor pentatonic scale, which is based mostly out of seventh position. He also includes a lower extension to the shape, which is shown below with the grey dot.

**E Minor Pentatonic Scale**
**(w/ lower extension)**

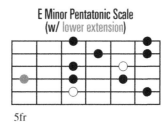

5fr

Aside from the generous bending display in measure 58, Clapton also serves up a relic from years gone by with the inclusion of the *major 7th* (D♯, fret 8 on string 3). This note is not part of the E minor pentatonic scale, but it sounds great nonetheless. Clapton no doubt picked up this sound from the great Delta slide players of the '30s and '40s, as it was much more common in that day and age.

In measure 59, notice how he slides down from fret 9 to fret 7 with the ring finger into the lower extension of this scale form. Why is this done? Well, one could argue that the sound of the slide is cool, which is true. But it also allows one to descend comfortably down to the tonic E note without having to stretch out for the 10th fret on string 5. For non-pinky players like Clapton, that tends to be a little uncomfortable. So basically, these extended forms of the minor pentatonic greatly aid in the ability to avoid the pinky!

## Section E – Straight-Eighths Boogie Riff

For section E, we shift to a straight-eighth feel, as opposed to the shuffle that pervades the rest of the song. This is very similar to the ensemble riff of Section B in that the same material is transposed almost verbatim for each of the I (E), IV (A), and V (B) chords. As in the B section, Clapton applies a slight *palm mute* here to keep the notes crisp and rhythmic. This is achieved by allowing your right-hand palm to touch the strings just in front of the bridge as you pick. The farther in you move from the bridge, the more muted the sound will be.

Again, there are minor variations notated in the music, but don't get bogged down with these. The spirit of the riff is essentially the same throughout each measure, even if Eric did occasionally pick one more string at a certain spot in different measures.

## Section F – Outro Guitar Solo

Section F kicks off a three-chorus guitar solo that takes the tune out. Eric really turns up the heat in this section, working again out of the 12th position E minor pentatonic. Notice that he starts with a unison bend—the way he did in Section C—but this time it's on a higher string set and really screams. In measures 77–79, he diverges a bit from the normal and bends fret 13 on string 3 up a half step to reach the A note of the underlying harmony. Use your middle finger for this and don't overreach the target pitch.

Eric kicks off the second chorus in measure 85 by strumming a four-string E chord in straight triplets, goosing the rhythm section on with increased fury. He plows through the rest of the chorus with more poignant licks from the E minor pentatonic.

At the beginning of the third chorus, Clapton fakes us out a bit, as it sounds as though he's going to recap the main theme an octave higher than in the beginning. He quickly abandons the idea in measure 100, though, when he shifts up to the upper extension box in 15th position for some soaring bends. Sometimes called the "Albert King box," this is a small box form extending the standard minor pentatonic box that, like the B.B. box, only occupies the top three strings. In the key of E in this higher octave, it would look like this:

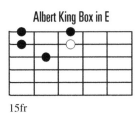

Albert King Box in E

15fr

In measure 101, Clapton slips back down to the 12th-fret position and rides out the rest of the song there. At 107, as is custom in blues tunes, the band stops and allows Slowhand to take them home with a lick that harkens a bit back to the triplet hammer-on lick from the main theme. The notes are different here, but they come from the E major pentatonic scale and convey the appropriate spirit. In traditional blues ending fashion, Clapton pounds it into the ground with the half-step move of F7 to E7, which is similar to what he did in measure 7 from Section A. Phew… what a ride!

Hide Away
Full Song

# HIDE AWAY
## By Freddie King and Sonny Thompson

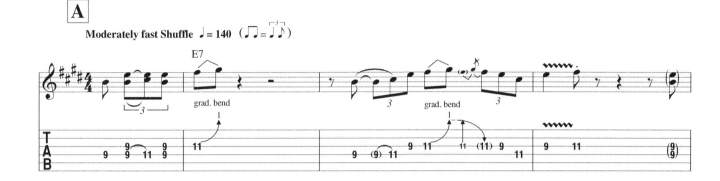

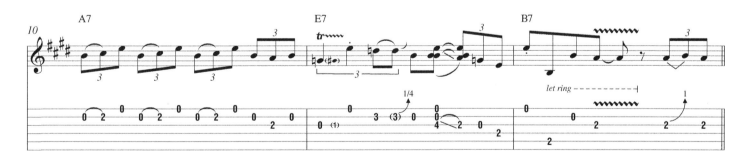

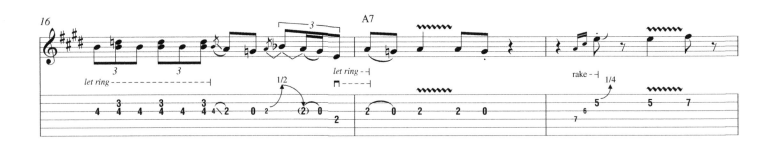

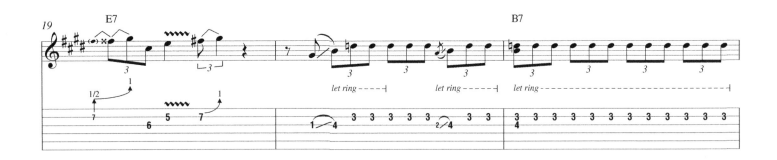

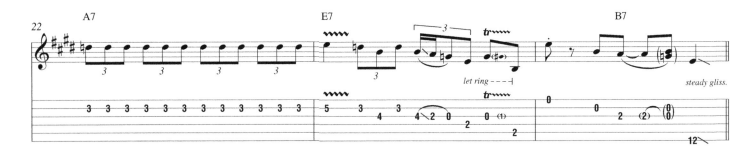

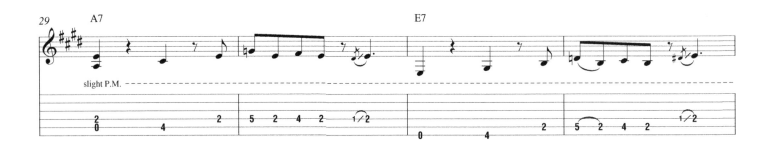

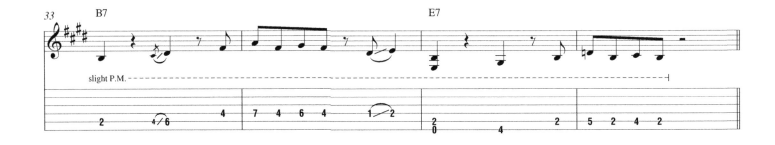

*Played as even eighths.

**Played behind the beat.

**Played behind the beat.

***Played ahead of the beat. *Played as even eighths.

***Played ahead of the beat.

*Played as even eighths.

# Cross Road Blues (Crossroads)
## From *Wheels of Fire*, 1968

You can't really overestimate the influence of Cream's recording of "Crossroads." Stripping away the subsequent influence of Clapton's guitar work on this track, you're still left with this incredible fact: with this recording, Cream almost single-handedly resurrected interest in Robert Johnson's music. He certainly had a good deal of help from the Rolling Stones as well (with "Love in Vain"), but this is where it all started. Of course, stripping away Clapton's influence on the guitar world with regard to this track is simply not possible. In a word, it's immense. It's as far-reaching as any song at this point, and it continues to inspire countless players nearly 50 years later.

In case you've never heard Robert Johnson's original recording of this song, you'd be in for quite a shock if you did. Cream's version sounds absolutely nothing like it, and the fact that it's an electrified band playing what was originally a vocal/acoustic song is only the beginning. Whereas the original lopes along in a slow shuffle, Cream's version rides along in a speedy, straight-eighth groove. Whereas Johnson's vocal delivery was serpentine and heavy on inflection, Clapton's is succinct and clipped. Aside from changing the chords or the lyrics (and Clapton actually does change a few here and there), Cream couldn't really do much more to make it their own. For reference, the song transcription begins on page 28.

### Intro
The song kicks of with the main riff of the song, which is based on an open A chord.

After an initial chordal attack on beat 1, Clapton alternates fret 2 on string 3 with the open string 3 to create the song's simple, yet insanely catchy hook. The rhythm becomes syncopated on beat 3, as 16th-note subdivisions are introduced into the alternating A and G notes, and the one-measure riff comes to a close with a low C note on string 5 at fret 3 that's bent a quarter step. This becomes the go-to riff for the A chord between the vocal lines throughout the entire song, so take your time with it and be sure you've got it down before proceeding. Notice how, in measure 3, Clapton harmonizes with himself in ultra-cool fashion by adding the second string to form the dyads of A/C# and G/B. How cool is that?

For the D7 chord in measures 5–6, Clapton arpeggiates through an open-position D7 voicing. Notice that he keeps things fairly spacious here as to not get too muddy.

For the E chord in measure 9, he sticks to a basic E5 shape on the bottom three strings.

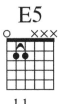

At measure 10, however, he abandons chording altogether and launches into a speedy A minor pentatonic lick based out of the fifth position box form that quickly turns into a composite scale, as the major 3rd (C♯) is liberally included as well. The scale form would look like this, with the major 3rd indicated in grey.

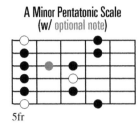

A Minor Pentatonic Scale
(w/ optional note)

5fr

For the lick beginning on beat 2 of measure 11, begin by hammering from your index finger on fret 5 of string 3 to your middle on fret 6. Because of the "let ring" notation, you can then simply barre strings 2 and 1 with your index finger. The rest of the measure lays out perfectly if you're a pinky user. If not, you'll need to stretch a bit to grab fret 8 with your ring finger.

## Verse

For the verse, Clapton reverts to the traditional boogie-style 5ths/6ths pattern (using a palm mute), respective to each chord, save for the spots after each vocal phrase, where he returns to the main hook (without palm mute). Here's how each boogie pattern looks:

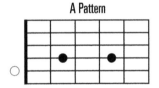

A Pattern

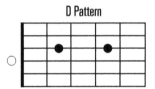

D Pattern

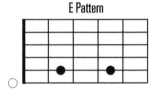

E Pattern

## Guitar Solo 1

After the second verse, Clapton breaks into his first solo of the song. Wisely, he keeps it relatively lower in range, which allows him room to move up for the famous and climactic second solo. He begins working out of the A major pentatonic scale form in second position, which looks exactly like an F♯ minor box shape.

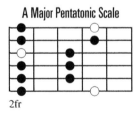

A Major Pentatonic Scale

2fr

Notice the famous vibrato he applies to the repeated tonic A notes at fret 2 on string 3 with the index finger. It's almost as if he's revving his engine for the ensuing take-off. Of note is the bright-sounding C♯ at fret 6, string 3 over the D chord, at which Clapton arrives via a ring-finger slide from the 4th fret. Aside from being a colorful note, it also serves the purpose of relocating his hand to the fifth position, where he spends the majority of the next four measures. He's working here out of the basic A minor pentatonic box, but it's more of a composite scale, as he also includes notes from the major pentatonic. Taken altogether, the scale formed would look something like this:

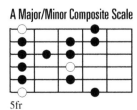

A Major/Minor Composite Scale

5fr

In measure 33, Clapton sneaks up to the seventh position by way of a ring-finger slide from fret 7 to 9 on the third string. This is a common blues move used heavily by players like Billy Gibbons. To master this move, try repeating this exercise. Use your index finger for fret 5, string 3 and your middle finger for fret 8, string 2. Everything else should be played with the ring finger. Make sure all the notes are speaking clearly.

Crossroads
Example 1

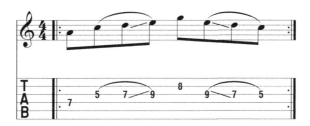

In measure 35, we see another classic sliding move. After playing the A note on fret 5 of string 1, Clapton slides up to the same note on string 2 at fret 10. He does this with his ring finger, which puts him in eighth position and what's commonly known as the A minor pentatonic extended box, which looks like this:

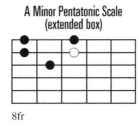

A Minor Pentatonic Scale
(extended box)

8fr

After a few licks in the extended box, notice how Clapton slips back down to the fifth position with a descending slide from fret 9 to 7 on string 3. This is performed with the middle finger, so right afterward, you'll need to reach back just a bit to grab the 5th fret with your index finger. This can be a little tricky at first, so try this exercise to isolate the move. Be sure to follow the indicated left-hand (LH) fingering exactly; otherwise you won't get the benefit of the exercise.

Crossroads
Example 2

For his next solo chorus, Clapton ramps up the intensity a bit and moves up to another scale form based around 12th and 13th position. For reference, the complete A minor pentatonic form in that position would look like this:

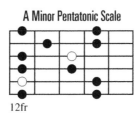

A Minor Pentatonic Scale

12fr

In practice, however, Clapton rarely (if ever) plays the scale form exactly as shown here when it comes to the lower strings. Rather, he'll slide down to 10th position when reaching the lower strings, which creates more of this scale form:

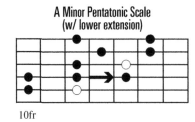

A Minor Pentatonic Scale
(w/ lower extension)

10fr

This allows him to traverse the entire range of this scale form without having to use his pinky. It also results in some cool-sounding slides to and from 10th position. In measures 40, 41, and the first half of 42, Clapton's working in 13th position, using his index finger for the 13th fret, his middle for fret 14 on string 3, and his ring finger for the 15th fret. For the second half of measure 42, he shifts to 12th position for the hammered double stop, quickly shifts down to the lower extension via a ring finger slide on string 4 at the beginning of measure 43, and then returns to 12th position in that same measure with another ring finger slide.

He spends the next several measures doing more of the same, throwing in a gritty unison bend in measure 44 and alternating the tonic A note at fret 14, string 3 with the bright major 7th (G#) on fret 13, string 3 in measure 47. This is a throwback to the sound of Delta blues slide players, who would perform this move often using the slide.

At measure 49, Clapton uses the ring finger to slide up a whole step from 12th position to 14th, accessing the A major pentatonic scale form there:

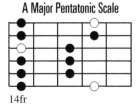

A Major Pentatonic Scale

14fr

It's interesting to note that these final phrases are very similar to his opening lines, only up an octave. As such, he bookends his improvisation intelligently and thematically.

## Guitar Solo 2

For the second solo, Clapton holds nothing back. He comes right out the gate as if he's possessed, launching into a rhythmic unison bend lick that just about peels your face off. He's working out of the A minor pentatonic box shape in the upper octave, which puts him in 17th position. Though he thoroughly entrenches himself in that position, he does add several key notes to the minor pentatonic scale to form a composite major/minor blues scale. Taken altogether, it would look like this (the added notes are in grey):

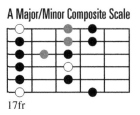

A Major/Minor Composite Scale

17fr

Due to the cramped quarters, you may want to try using your middle finger for the 19th fret and the ring for the 20th, the way Clapton would, throughout this section. If you're not used to bending with your middle finger much, this could be a bit awkward at first, because you're going to be bending fret 19 on string 3 a whole bunch. Occasionally, as with the double-stop bends in measure 77, you may want to use the ring finger for the 19th fret if the middle feels too awkward.

Other than that, there are a few quick string skips that you need to be ready for, such as the ones in measures 56, 63, and 84. But mostly he's just tearing that scale pattern up, down, sideways, in, and out. This type of fluidity just comes from years and years of experience and practice. That's all there is to it.

## Outro Verse

Clapton picks back up where he left off for the final verse, supporting his vocals with boogie 5th/6th riffs and the main hook over the A chord between vocal lines. When he reaches the IV chord (D) in the 10th bar of the form (measure 98 in the song), he hits a nice D7/F# voicing on the downbeat and stops with the rest of the band as he sings the final line.

After the final vocal line, he joins bassist Jack Bruce for a unison line played in the open-position A minor pentatonic scale. The full form looks like this:

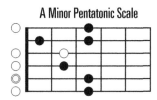

With regard to the fingering of this line, try using your index finger and middle finger for the 2nd-fret notes to see which you like best. Most likely, one method will feel more comfortable. Clapton finishes off with a composite blues lick in fifth position very similar to the one he used in measure 38, where it functioned as a turnaround lick.

**Crossroads Full Song**

# CROSS ROAD BLUES (CROSSROADS)

## Words and Music by Robert Johnson

**Intro**
**Moderately fast Rock** ♩ = 130

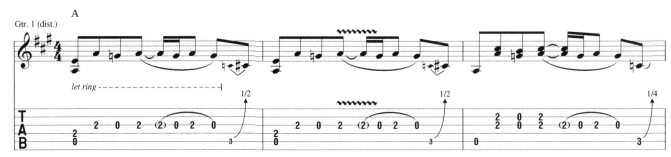

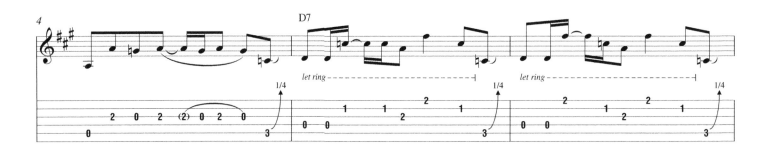

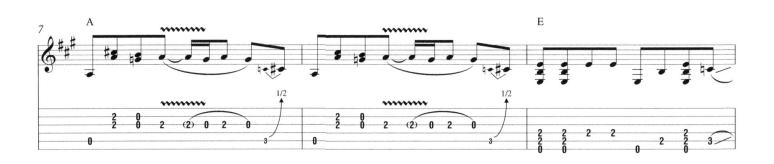

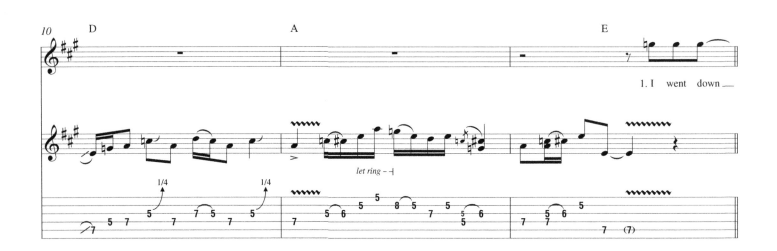

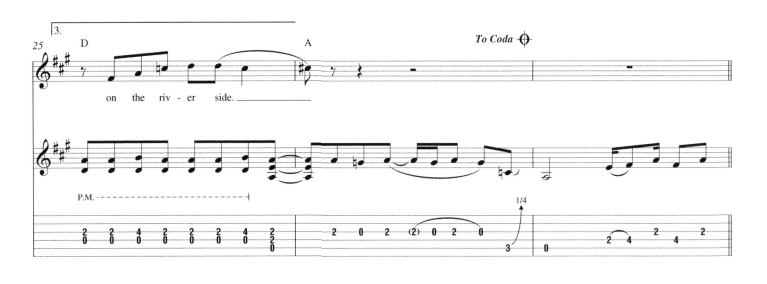

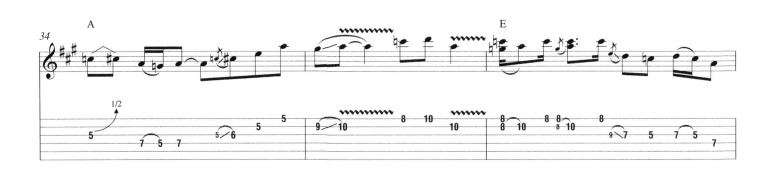

Outro-Verse

5. You can run, you can run, tell my friend, boy, Wil-lie Brown. ___

*Additional Lyrics*

2. I went down to the crossroad, tried to flag a ride.
   Down to the crossroad, tried to flag a ride.
   Nobody seemed to know me. Ev'rybody passed me by.

3. When I'm goin' down to Rosedale, take my rider by my side.
   Goin' down to Rosedale, take my rider by my side.
   We can still barrelhouse, baby, on the riverside.

# *Badge*
## From *Goodbye*, 1969

Cream burned brightly and fiercely for the few years that they existed in the late '60s, and they changed the music world forever in the process, cementing the power trio, along with Jimi Hendrix, as an archetype in the rock world. Their final album, 1969's *Goodbye*, was short and sweet and is divided in half with three live tracks and three studio tracks. Each member contributed one song to the studio side, and Clapton turned in one of his best in "Badge," which was co-written with his good friend George Harrison.

A moody, steady rocker, "Badge" contains some stellar rhythm guitar work by co-writer George Harrison and one of the most inspired leads of Clapton's career. Let's check it out. For reference, the song transcription begins on page 40.

## Intro

The song begins with Harrison on rhythm and Jack Bruce on bass. Harrison plays very rhythmically through the Am–D chord progression, alternating muted strums with unmuted ones. He's using two barre chord forms here:

For the "X" strums, simply release the pressure with your fret hand so that you're still making contact with the strings but not pressing them down (see photos). When you strum, you should hear nothing but a dead, percussive clicking sound.

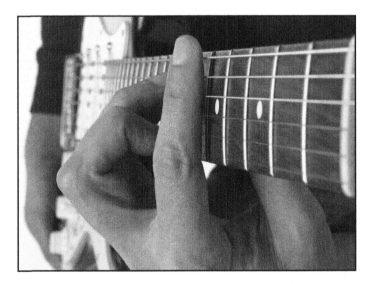
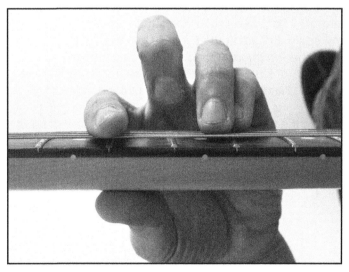

Notice how he quickly establishes a pattern of dead strums on the downbeats and normal strums on the upbeats. Also realize that the dead strums are accented much more than the chord strums, which are almost inaudible by comparison. To get this down, practice this exercise. Use downstrokes on the downbeats and upstrokes on the upbeats. Start slowly at first and then build up to the tempo of the song.

**Badge**
**Example 1**

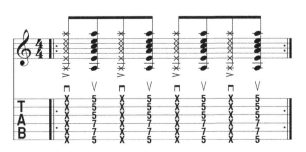

## Verse

Ginger Baker enters on drums for the verse, and things are fully under way. Harrison begins in a similar fashion to the intro, but he soon moves to full strums exclusively as the progression reaches the new chords of Esus2 and Em in measures 5–6.

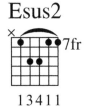

Esus2

1 3 4 1 1

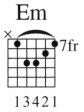

Em

1 3 4 2 1

Notice that the only difference between these two chords is the addition of your middle finger on fret 8, string 2 for the Em chord.

After repeating the same four-bar phrase in measures 7–10, we see a new chord progression of C–Am–Bm7–Am(add9) to round out the verse. Harrison strums these all as some kind of barre chord, with the exception of the Bm7, which appears as only a partial chord on the top three strings.

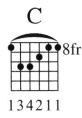

C

1 3 4 2 1 1

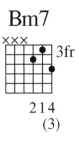

Bm7

2 1 4
(3)

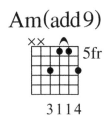

Am(add9)

3 1 1 4

Notice that two possible fingerings are shown for the Bm7 chord. I highly recommend the first (with the pinky on string 1), because this allows you to use the pinky as a guide finger for the following Am(add9) chord, which is not the easiest chord in the world to just grab out of nowhere. Just before the repeat of the verse, Harrison walks back up to the Am chord (along with the bass) on the low E string. The tempo is probably slow enough here that fingering isn't a terrible concern. I tend to play fret 3 with the index, fret 4 with the middle, and then shift up to fifth position for the Am chord. But you could also use the index finger for all of the notes without too much trouble.

During the latter part of the second verse, during the C–Am–Bm–Am(add9) progression, Harrison lets loose with a series of Hendrix-like chordal embellishments. For the C chord, he slides up to a first-inversion form in fifth position. Start with fret 3 on string 5 with the index finger and then slide from fret 5 to 7 with the ring finger to reach fifth position.

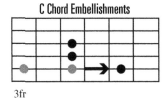

C Chord Embellishments

3fr

Next, on beat 3 of measure 16, while barring strings 4 and 3 at the 5th fret with your index finger, quickly hammer on to fret 7 with your ring finger. Be careful not to touch the third string when you do this so that it rings out as well. Leave your first finger barred as you finish out the rest of the measure.

In measure 17, Harrison decorates the Am chord with a B note at fret 7 on string 1 that's hammered from fret 5. The difficult thing about this is that, since your ring finger is fretting the A note on string 4 (fret 7), you'll have to hammer on to the B on string 1 with your pinky. Here's an exercise that can help you out on this move and the previous one on the C chord. Start slowly and then work up the speed:

Badge
Example 2

For the Bm chord in measure 18, Harrison performs a similar hammering move to the one in measure 16, except this time he's in seventh position, he's moved up to strings 3 and 2, and he pulls off after the hammer-on to form a 16th-note triplet. Don't worry too much about touching the second string when you pull off from fret 9 to fret 7 on the third string; the move goes by so quickly that it's negligible. But be sure to start slowly so that the hammer-pull combination itself is clean. Also pay attention to the staccato markings throughout this phrase; they play a big part in the rhythmic sound.

After sustaining the Am(add9) chord again, as with the end of the first verse, we reach the song's signature arpeggio riff. There seems to be great debate over whether this part was actually played by Harrison or Clapton on the original recording. It certainly seems to have Harrison's stamp on it, because he played some very similar figures on the Beatles' *Abbey Road*, which was recorded shortly after *Goodbye*. There are three guitars on the song, so there was definitely an overdubbed part. Nevertheless, be sure and listen to the audio and follow along with this riff on paper before trying to play it; it can be a little tricky because of the *syncopation*—i.e., the stress of the upbeats. After the pickup notes D, F♯, and A, which form a D major arpeggio, arpeggiate through these basic chord forms (not all of these notes are always picked, but these are the chord forms):

G/C

G/B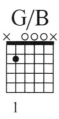

G

As mentioned, the G/C and G/B chords begin on an upbeat, so it can feel a little tricky at first. Regarding the picking, you'll need to try various approaches to see what feels most comfortable.

## Bridge

This new arpeggio riff becomes the basis for the song's bridge and is joined by Harrison playing some accenting chords on the lower strings. For the most part, he sticks to these forms:

C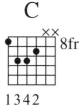

G/B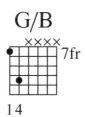

G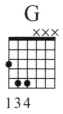

D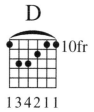

## Guitar Solo

The bridge leads way to the guitar solo—certainly one of the finest moments of Clapton's career, let alone the entire world of rock guitar. His ideas simply flowed as effortlessly as a river here, combining an incredibly strong rhythmic delivery, unpredictable leaps, and an absolutely killer tone. For the most part, Clapton's phrases are divided into three distinct positions on the fretboard, which we'll talk about along the way.

He begins working out of what appears to be the classic D minor pentatonic box in 10th position. In a virtuosic bending display, he combines precise pre-bends and releases during his pickup phrase in measure 34. If you've never tried pre-bends before, this is as good of a time as any. They're not the easiest thing in the world, so try this exercise before attempting the lick. You'll need to silently bend the 13th fret on string 2 up a whole step, pick it, and then release the appropriate amount. The whole-step release is easy, but the half-step release takes much more skill. Check your pitch against unbent notes to make sure you're on.

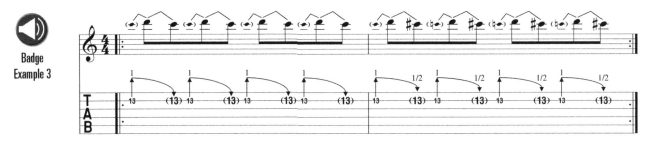

Badge
Example 3

What follows is just some incredibly soulful playing. Though he spends much time in the minor pentatonic scale, it's not long before he begins to add other notes to form a composite scale that includes some major sounds as well. If we gather all the tones he uses in this position, we end up with this as a scale form:

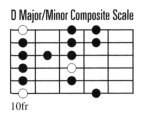

In measure 37, he pulls off some more pre-bend magic, alternating between whole- and half-step bends on fret 13 of string 1 with pinpoint accuracy. Notice throughout how he toys with the minor 3rd (F) and major 3rd (F♯) on string 1 by way of different bends.

In measure 40, he slides up from fret 12 to 15 on the second string to the extended box in 13th position, which looks like this:

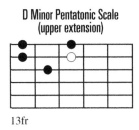

More bending madness ensues there, as he combines whole-, half-, and quarter-step bends on frets 13 and 15 with the index and ring fingers, respectively. In measure 45, he slides up to fret 16 on the third string with his middle finger, which places him in 15th position—also known as the "B.B. King box."

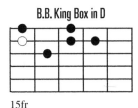

On beat 3 of measure 43, you'll need to bend fret 17 on string 2 and, while holding that bend, play fret 17 on string 1, and then pick string 2 again and release the bend.

Make sure that you're holding the bend steadily as you pick the note on string 1, as it can have a tendency to fall a bit if you're not careful. Try this exercise to get it down. After bending the 17th fret on beat 1, keep it there until the release on beat 4.

Badge
Example 4

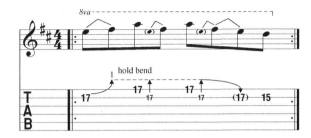

In measure 46, he briefly climbs up to the 19th fret for some more bending madness before, in measure 47, passing briefly through the B.B. box (beat 2) and the extended box (beat 3) en route to the standard box in 10th position for the final composite phrase. This solo isn't particularly difficult (though it's certainly not easy), but its fluidity, vibe, and energy are truly engaging, and that's what makes it so memorable.

## Outro Verse

For the final verse, Clapton fills in the holes left by the vocals with some gorgeous lines mostly based out of the E minor pentatonic scale in 12th position:

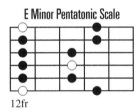

E Minor Pentatonic Scale

12fr

Note, however, that he does dress things up in measure 52 by adding the 9th (F♯) on fret 14, string 1 and by sliding into the B on fret 12, string 2 from a half step below. In measures 55–56, he plays another pre-bend phrase that descends down into the lower extension position of the E minor pentatonic, which looks like this:

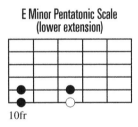

E Minor Pentatonic Scale
(lower extension)

10fr

This is a really common move in blues and rock and allows non-pinky players such as Clapton to avoid fretting the low G note on string 6 at fret 15, which would normally require a bit of a stretch. Instead, they can slide down and maintain the index/ring pairing.

To bring things to a close, in measure 59 Clapton plays a nice double-stop riff in 10th position. Slide into fret 11 on the third string with your middle finger, barre your first finger for the 10th-fret double stops, and use either a ring-finger barre or your ring and pinky for the 12th-fret double stops. Over the final Am chord, the B/E double stop at fret 12 sounds particularly lovely, as the B note functions as the chord's 9th. It makes quite a fitting end to a guitar tour de force.

# BADGE

### Words and Music by Eric Clapton and George Harrison

Badge
Full Song

**Bridge**

Gtr. 2: w/ Rhy. Fig. 1 (5 times)

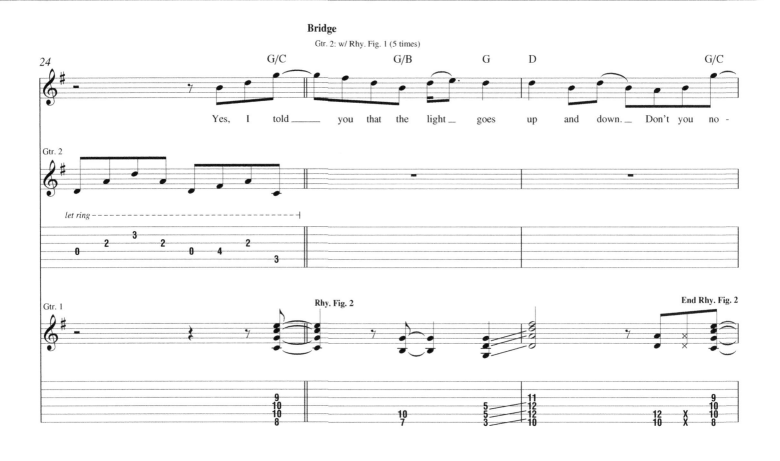

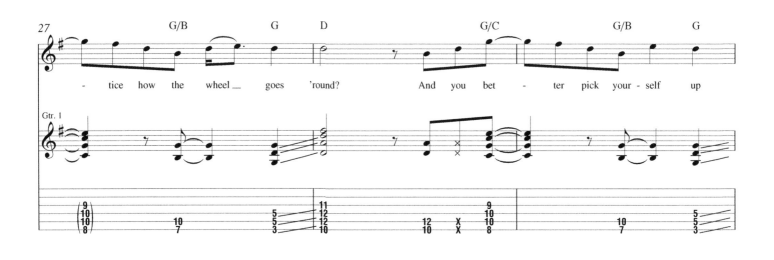

**Guitar Solo**

Gtr. 1: w/ Rhy. Fig. 2 (6 times)
Gtr. 2: w/ Rhy. Fig. 1 (6 times)

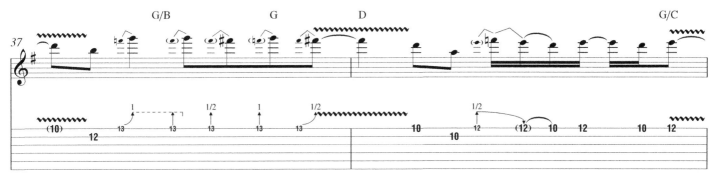

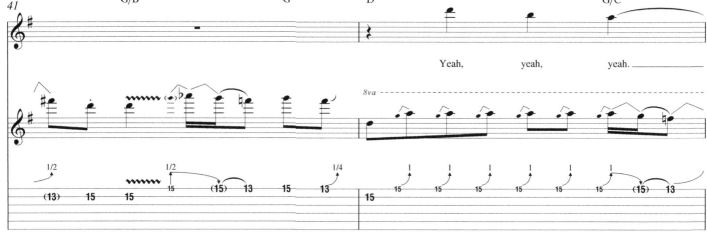

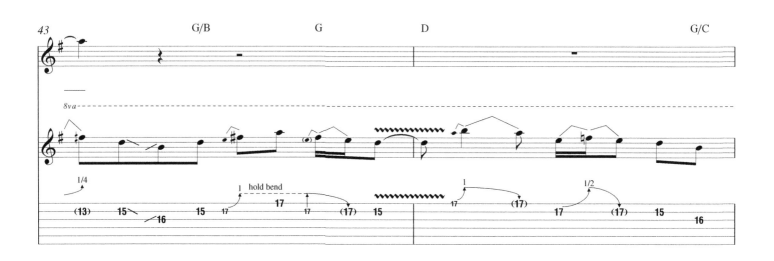

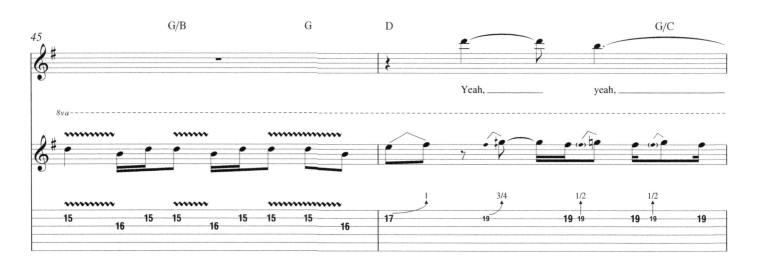

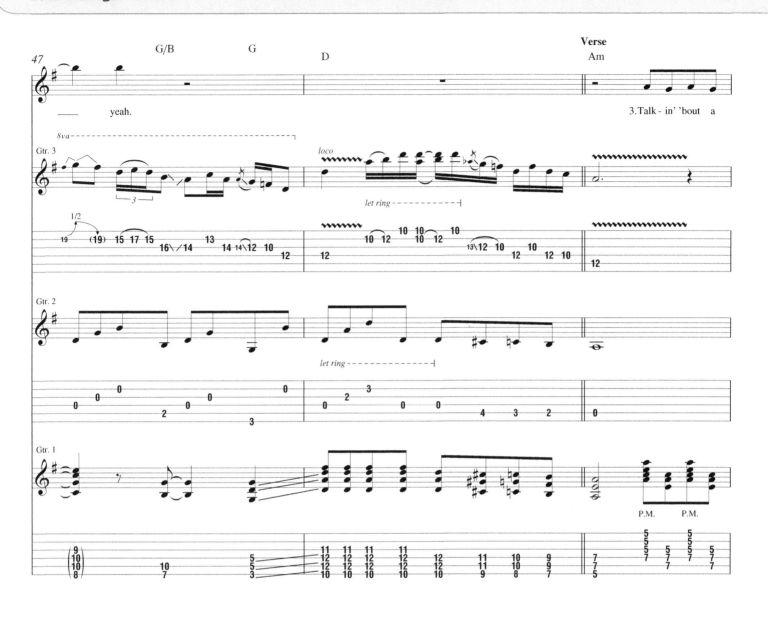

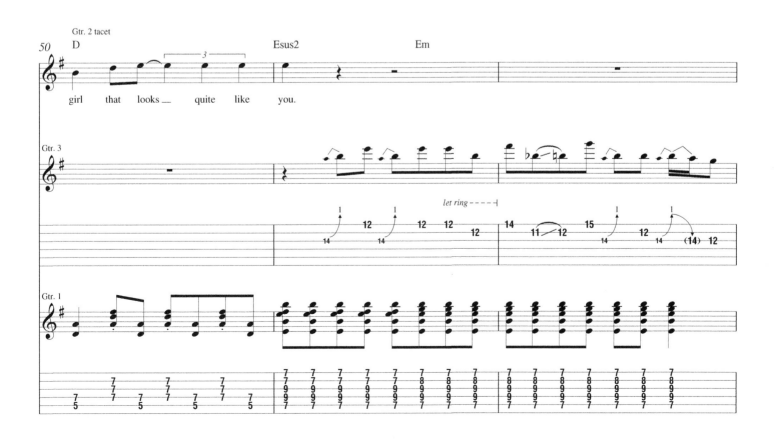

*Additional Lyrics*

2. I told you not to wander 'round in the dark.
   I told you 'bout the swans, that they live in the park.
   Then I told you 'bout our kid, now he's married to Mable.

# Bell Bottom Blues
## From *Layla and Other Assorted Love Songs*, 1970

After the intense spotlight that fell upon both Cream and his next project, Blind Faith (with Steve Winwood and Ginger Baker), Clapton had had enough and longed for some privacy. He recruited a few members from Delaney & Bonnie, with whom he had toured briefly, and set out to quietly record what would become *Layla and Other Assorted Love Songs*. The addition of slide guitar master Duane Allman to the sessions proved to seemingly elevate Clapton to another level himself, resulting in some of his most inspired performances on record.

Along with the title track, "Bell Bottom Blues" (which was, along with the title track, also written about his unrequited love for Patti Boyd, wife of George Harrison) has proved itself an immortal classic and contains some of Clapton's finest guitar work to date. For reference, the song transcription begins on page 52.

## Intro

Clapton kicks the intro off with a pickup phrase that suggests a G harmony (the V chord in the key of C). Although it would be easy to do, notice that the C note at string 5, fret 3 is not allowed to ring through, as this would somewhat weaken the effect of the G harmony. Instead, it functions as a passing tone en route to the open D string. On the downbeat proper, Clapton begins slowly arpeggiating through the chords in eighth notes, backed quietly by drums, bass, and organ. The tempo here is slow enough so that picking is not a concern; the bigger issue is making sure you play in time. Slow tempos can be deceptively tricky in this regard. Though not all of these strings are picked, here are the full chords from which these arpeggios are derived:

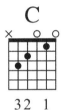  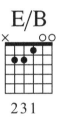   

At the end of the intro, in measure 4, two other guitars enter, playing similar lead lines that begin somewhat in unison and break into harmony at the end. For Gtr. 2, you can begin with a partial ring-finger barre at fret 13 for the first two notes, use the index finger for fret 11 on string 2, and bend the 12th fret on string 3 with the middle finger. (That's the way Clapton would do it, anyway.) Gtr. 3 would start the same way, though you'd obviously barre fret 11 with the index finger to catch both notes. After bending the 12th fret, hold it, play fret 13 on string 2 with the ring finger, and then pick string 3 again, releasing the bend and adding vibrato. Beneath this, Gtr. 1 strums Fmaj7 and G7 chords, accenting the same rhythms as the leads.

## Verse

Gtr. 1 continues playing the same thing as the intro for the verse, while Gtrs. 2 & 3 add fills between the vocal phrases. In measure 6, Gtr. 2 works out of fifth position in the A minor pentatonic box for a fill:

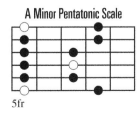

A Minor Pentatonic Scale
5fr

In measure 10, Gtr. 2 moves up to the octave position of the A minor pentatonic box in 17th position for a similar fill.

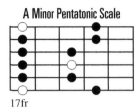

**A Minor Pentatonic Scale**

17fr

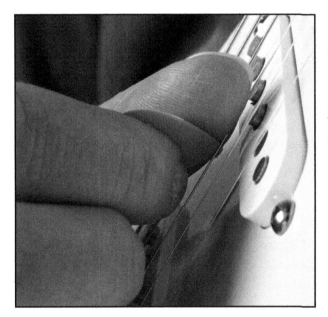

Note the "semi-P.H." in the music; this stands for "semi pinch harmonic." If Clapton were using a dirtier (more distorted) sound, this would probably sound closer to the pinch harmonic squeals of Billy Gibbons. To create this sound, choke up on the pick and allow your thumb to brush against the string at the same time you pick it (see photo). You should get a higher pitch than the normal fretted note. Depending on where you pick along the string, that higher pitch will change.

Simultaneously, Gtr. 3 adds a similar fill working out of the "B.B. box" in 13th position, which is based on the relative major, C major. This box has variations, but usually looks like this (as is evident in this lick, many of these notes can be bent varying degrees to reach other notes):

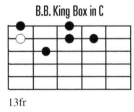

**B.B. King Box in C**

13fr

This M.O. of simultaneous fills from Gtrs. 2 & 3 continues through most of the song. They're panned on opposite sides of the stereo spectrum (though not hard panned), but it's still surprising how well the two never seem to get in each other's way.

## Pre-Chorus

The pre-chorus features a dramatic key change to A major, and Gtr. 1 continues playing chords. Notice that Clapton uses his thumb on string 6 for barre-type chords here.

In measure 13, Gtr. 2 plays a fill again out of the 17th-position A minor pentatonic box, making use of a very nifty *oblique bend* with strings 3 and 1. An oblique bend is a double stop in which one string is bent and the other is stationary. For this one, you'll need to bend fret 19 on string 3 up a whole step with the ring finger and, while holding that bend, play fret 17 on string 1 with your index finger.

Notice, however, that Clapton wisely resolves the line to C♯ at fret 18 on string 3 to coincide with the A chord harmony beneath. Working out of the upper extension A minor pentatonic box in eighth position, Gtr. 3 simultaneously plays a fill as well:

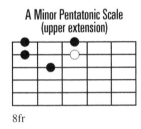

8fr

After bending fret 10 on string 1 up a whole step with the ring finger, Clapton releases it and makes an adjustment to the normal scale form, playing C♯ on fret 9 of string 1 instead of C at fret 8, again repurposing the lick to work over the key of A major. After moving down string 3 from fret 9 to 7 via a middle-finger slide, he again resolves the line to a C♯ note—this time fret 6 on string 3 (an octave below that of Gtr. 2).

The two guitars play similar figures in measure 15, but they maintain the intensity by failing to drop down to the lower register. This helps build momentum leading into the chorus.

## Chorus

The chorus remains in A major, but we see a new chord progression of A–Amaj7–A7–D–E. Gtr. 1 strums these chords in simple rhythms, relying on common, open-position chord shapes. Note that if you finger the A chords in this fashion, you can leave your second and third fingers in the same place for all three versions of the A:

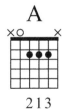
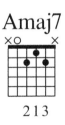
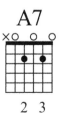

Over the top, Gtrs. 2 and 3 provide the real ear candy with similar lines on the higher strings that highlight the chromatically descending phrase of A–G♯–G that's present in the chord progression. These notes are pivoted against a high C♯ on fret 9, string 1 in a "ding-dong" bell-like fashion. Try starting in measure 16 with your middle finger for fret 9, string 1 and your ring finger on fret 10, string 2. You can keep your middle finger there while using your index finger to catch the 9th and 8th frets. For Gtr. 2 at the beginning of measure 18 (the 2/4 measure), slide from fret 9 to 10 with your ring finger and then quickly slide into fret 12 on string 4 with your middle finger. Use your ring finger for fret 12 on string 2 and then quickly slide up again to fret 16 on string 4 with your middle finger, using your index for the 15th fret on string 2. This move will take some practice, so start slowly and build up to speed.

## Verse 2

Verse 2 follows the format of verse 1 for the most part, but there are a few things that warrant some attention. In measure 26, Gtr. 3 plays a slightly different version of its F–G7 lick from the intro. You'll most likely use a partial barre for fret 13 in this lick. If you barre with your pinky, use your ring finger for the bend. If you barre with your ring finger, use your middle finger for the bend. Clapton would most likely do the latter, but try both to see which feels best for you.

Whichever method you choose, you'll need to bend string 3 and hold it while playing the barred second and first strings. Then you'll pick string 3 again and release the bend.

In measure 28, Gtr. 2 peels off a nice hammer-pull extravaganza that works its way down through almost all six strings. The actual hammering and pulling off isn't the hardest part of this lick; it's the planting of the index finger on the next string quickly and cleanly that's the issue. So take your time with it and make sure you're getting that right.

## Guitar Solo

Clapton's guitar solo is a study in understated beauty. After quoting the vocal melody for the pickup phrase in 12th position, he settles into an A minor pentatonic scale form (or the relative major, C major, if you'd like) based around mostly 12th and 13th position. He does, however, make use of a lower extension that brings him down to 10th position briefly. When you analyze all the notes, you end up with an extended scale form that looks like this:

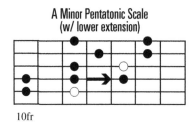

A Minor Pentatonic Scale
(w/ lower extension)

10fr

This form allows Clapton to use a slide to descend down to the lower octave A note (and the G below that), which works better with his preferred three-finger approach to lead playing. Clapton squeezes every bit of emotion out of this form by making use of tasteful bends at fret 15 on strings 2 and 1, both performed with the ring finger, not to mention a bluesy half-step bend at fret 12, string 4, also played with the ring finger. In measure 39, you can practically hear him weep as he bends and releases fret 15, string 2 in rhythm for nearly a whole measure, resisting the urge to restrike the string and milking it dry. For the final phrase in measures 40–41, he really chokes up on the pick and plays almost exclusively semi pinch harmonics, generating slightly different varying percentages of note vs. harmonic each time.

## Pre-Chorus 3

Just because the solo is over doesn't mean you have to stop playing, and Clapton demonstrates this with continuing lead lines over the following pre-chorus. He kicks things off with a staple of soul guitar: a 6th interval. Fret 9 on string 3 and string 1 create a major 6th interval, to be precise, and you'll no doubt recognize the sound from its use in songs like Sam & Dave's "Soul Man." Use the middle finger for string 3 and the ring finger for string 1 here. (Also check out "Hide Away" for a great lick using 6ths.)

He continues by falling down A major scale tones on string 3 by way of slides. This is a great way to traverse the neck in a very legato fashion. Try this exercise, in which we work through an entire octave of the A major scale on string 3, to get a feel for the technique:

Bell Bottom Blues
Example 1

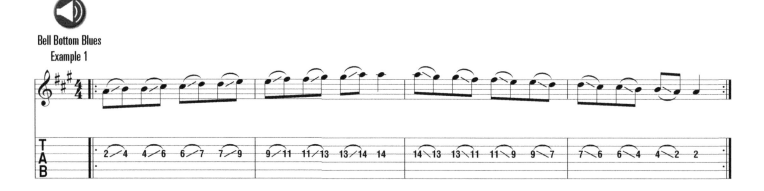

After a phrase from the A composite scale in fifth position, he leaps up to fret 12 on string 2, sliding up to fret 14 with his ring finger. He continues sliding up notes of the A major scale (in similar fashion to measure 42, when he slid down) until he reaches fret 17, which puts him in position for a phrase from the A major pentatonic scale in 14th position:

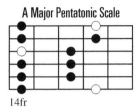

A Major Pentatonic Scale

14fr

He finishes it off with a lick in seventh position that begins by sliding your ring finger up to fret 9 on string 5. The rest of it should fall in place from there.

## Pre-Chorus 4

In measure 55, Clapton really lets it fly with a momentum-building repetitive lick from the 17th-position A minor pentatonic scale. Use a picking pattern of down, down-up, down, down-up, etc. for this lick, and don't rush it! It may sound counterintuitive to want to a rush a lick that's already pretty speedy, but it's not uncommon at all, especially when the moves are as repetitive as this. He closes off this section with Gtr. 2 in measure 57 performing a very similar pre-bending move to one from the "Badge" solo (transposed here to A, obviously). After bending fret 20, string 1 up a whole step with the ring finger, alternate pre-bending it a whole step and half step to get the awesome stuttering effect. Intonation is crucial here, so check yourself with unbent pitches!

# BELL BOTTOM BLUES

## Words and Music by Eric Clapton

Bell Bottom Blues
Full Song

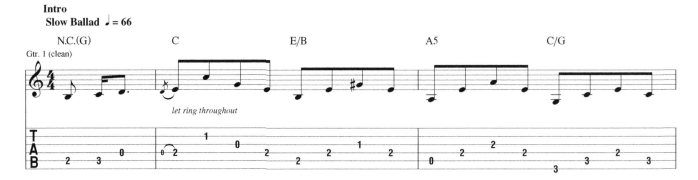

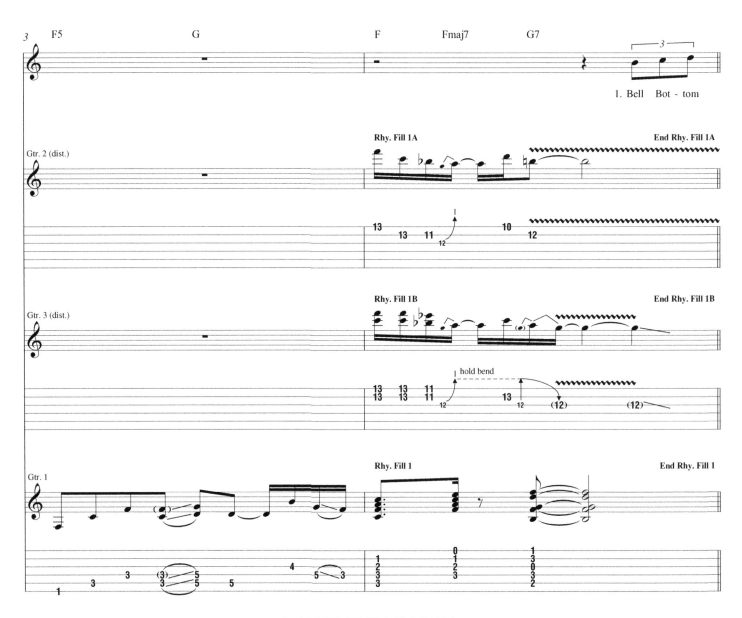

**Verse**

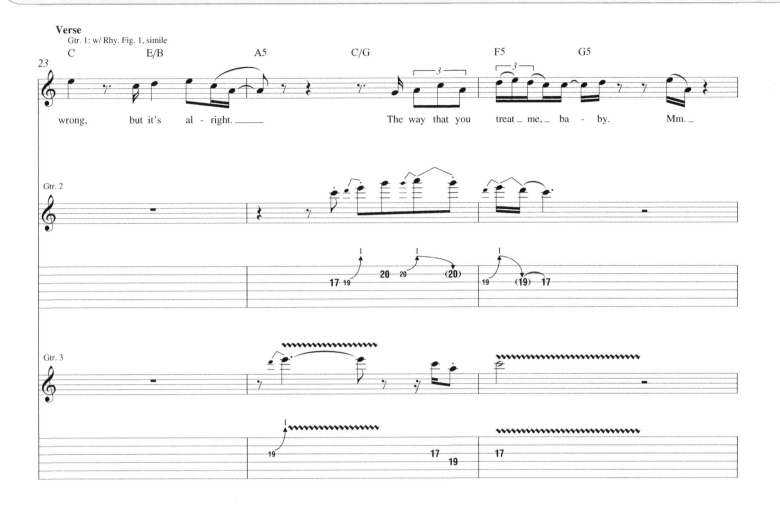

wrong, but it's al - right. _____ The way that you treat _ me, _ ba - by. Mm. _

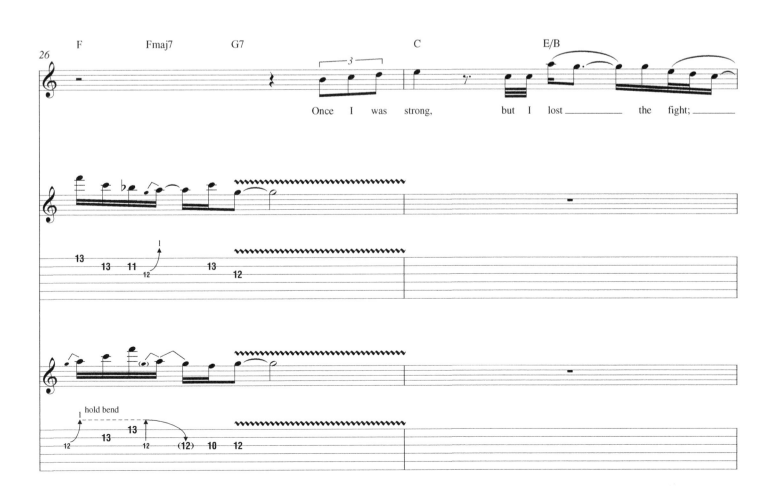

Once I was strong, but I lost _____ the fight; _____

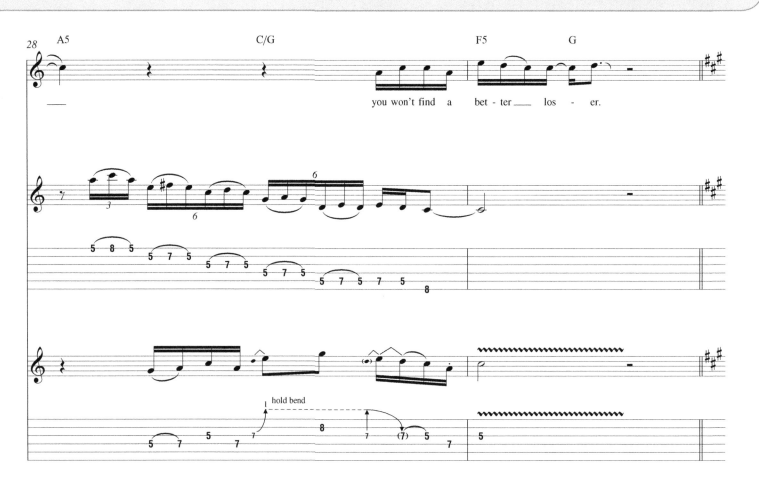

you won't find a bet - ter ___ los - er.

**Pre-Chorus**

Gtr. 1: w/ Rhy. Fig. 2, simile

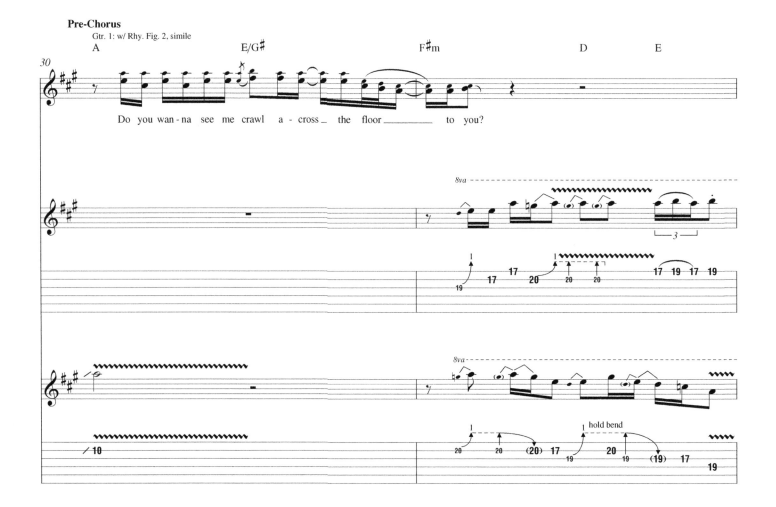

Do you wan - na see me crawl a - cross ___ the floor _____ to you?

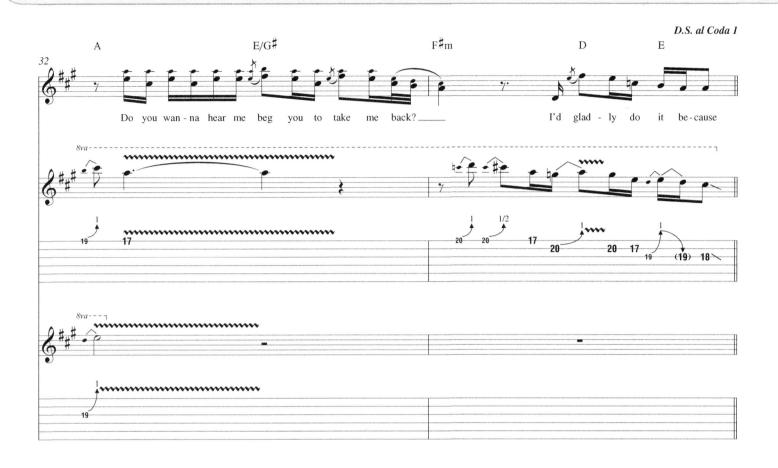

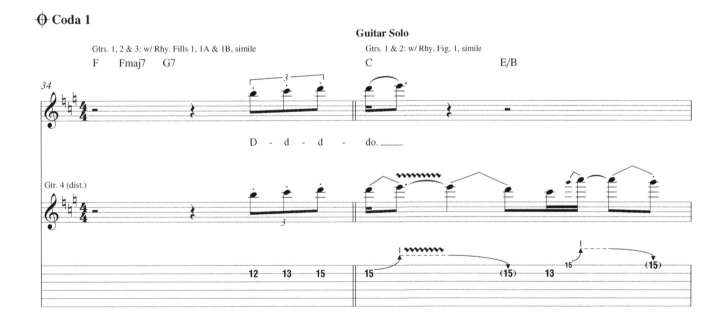

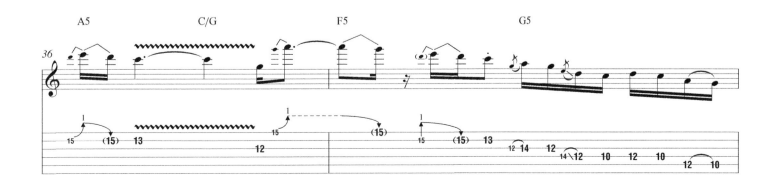

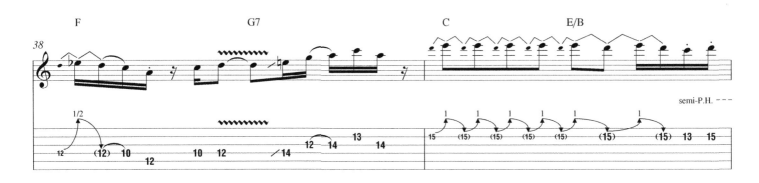

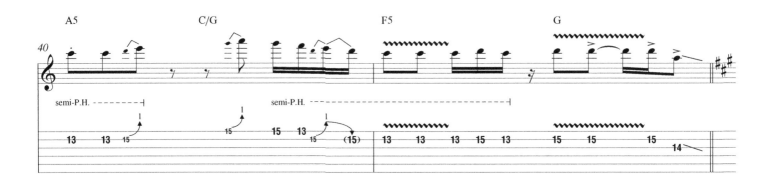

**Pre-Chorus**

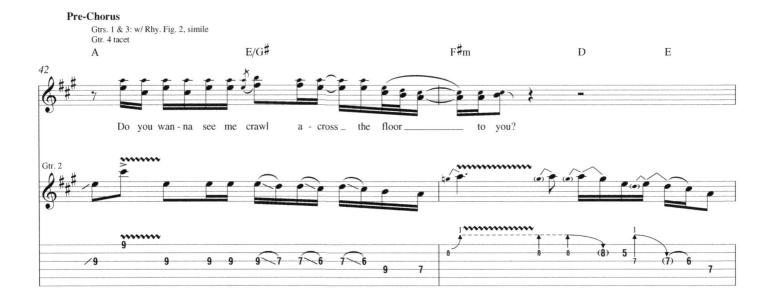

*D.S. al Coda 2*

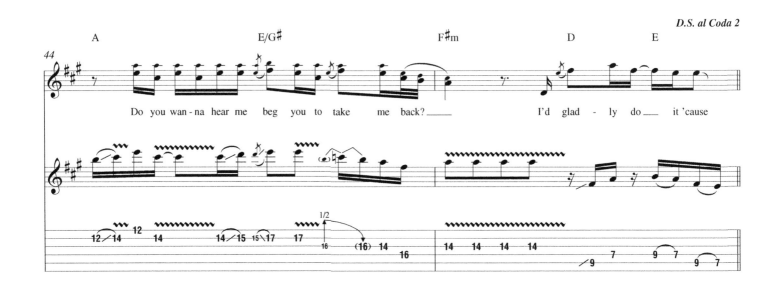

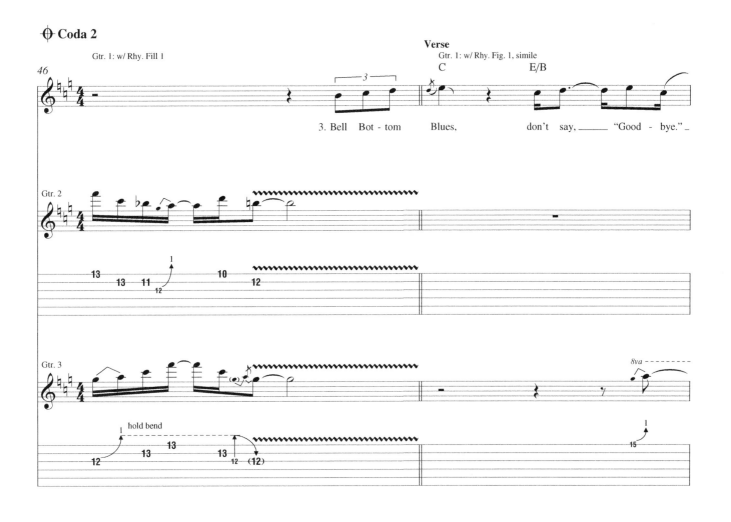

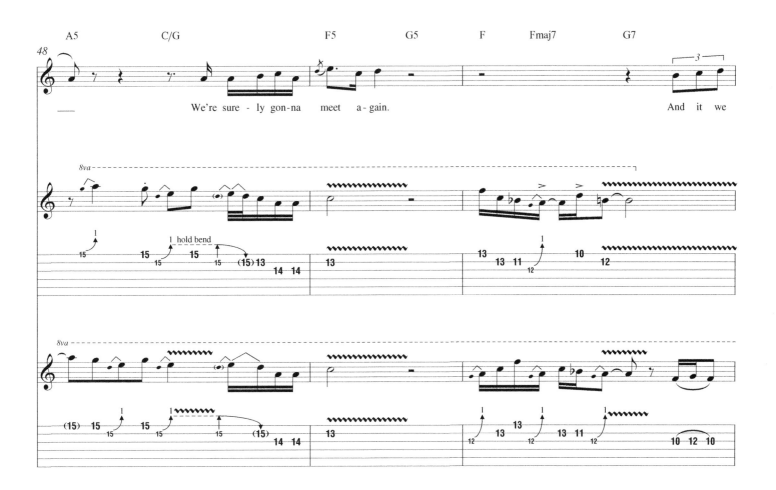

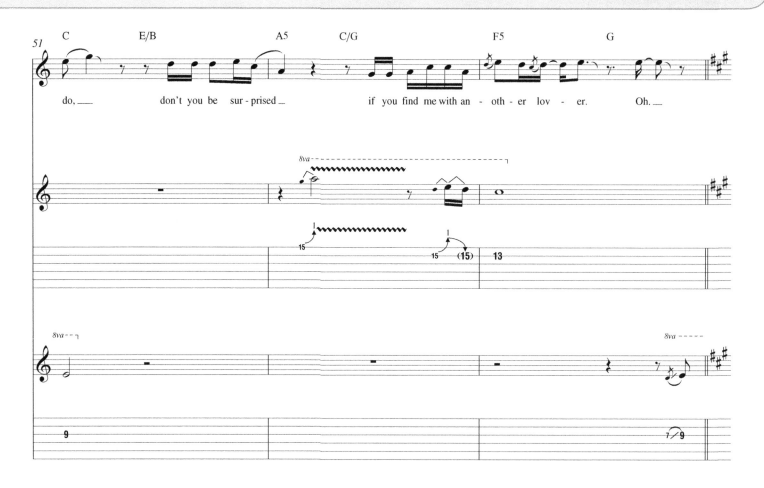

**Pre-Chorus**

Gtr. 1: w/ Rhy. Fig. 2, simile

# *Tears in Heaven*
## From *Unplugged*, 1992

Eric Clapton co-wrote "Tears in Heaven" with Will Jennings after the tragic loss of his four-year old son Conor, who fell out of a high-rise apartment window in New York in 1991. The song first appeared on the soundtrack to the movie *Rush*, for which Clapton wrote (or co-wrote) the entire score. It became a hit for him then, but it also enjoyed massive success when it was re-recorded for his 1992 *Unplugged* album. The latter version is the one we'll look at here. Clapton plays the song entirely fingerstyle, so you can lose that pick (for now, anyway). For reference, the song transcription begins on page 66.

## Intro

Clapton kicks off the song unaccompanied but is soon joined by second guitarist Andy Fairweather Low, who doubles Clapton almost verbatim for much of the song. After a low hammer-on from the open low E to fret 2 as a pickup, we're under way, and Clapton sounds most of the chord progression in A major by alternating plucked chords on the downbeats with bass notes on the upbeats. Notice the quick hammer-and-pull ornament he adds to the A chord, which is actually easier than it sounds. You'll use your middle finger for the move (the index will be barring). Just be sure that all three notes are clear and that you don't rush the hammer-pull combination. Here are the chord forms he mostly uses for this chord progression. Notice that Clapton uses his thumb on string 6 for the slash chords E/G♯ and D/F♯.

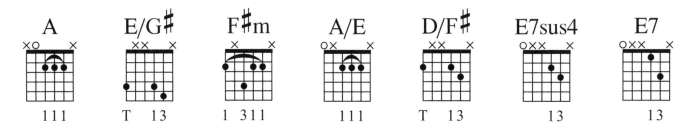

In case you're new to fingerpicking, try this exercise to get a feel for the basic comping pattern Clapton is using here. Use your thumb for the open A and E bass notes and your fingers for all the other notes.

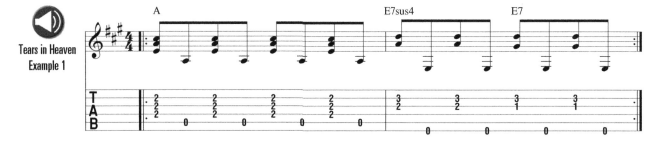

Tears in Heaven
Example 1

## Verse & Interlude

The verse begins in a very similar fashion as the intro, with Clapton making use of all the same chords, with only minor variation at times. Low begins by doubling Clapton, but in measure 2, over the F♯m chord, he breaks into a double-stop line on the higher strings comprised of mostly 4th intervals. Start with your ring finger on fret 5, string 2 and your pinky on fret 5, string 1 and slide both immediately up to fret 7. Use your index on fret 5 for the following A note. Beat 3 should be executed with your index on string 3 and your middle on string 2. Partially barre fret 2 on beat 4 with the index and use whichever feels comfortable for you on beat 4.5; it could be index on string 3 and middle on string 2 or several other combinations. The tempo is slow enough so that it's not terribly critical.

When the F♯m chord comes around again at measure 10, Low plays a different fill, this time based on 6th intervals. These could be fingered a number of ways, especially since he plays them all staccato, so try a variety of options until you find something that works. The one thing I will say is that it will most likely be easiest to partially barre strings 1–3 with the index on beat 3 and quickly hammer onto frets 6 and 5 with the ring and middle fingers, respectively. Regarding the pick hand, fingerpicking is the way to go here, with the thumb handling all the notes on string 3, and the index finger handling all the ones on string 1. You could also try other fingerings here, such as the more classical approach of index and ring fingers for strings 3 and 1, respectively (which keeps the fingers assigned to their usual strings).

At measure 13, a new progression shows up, and both guitarists play similar chording patterns. The new voicings that Clapton uses here are as follows:

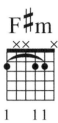    

The interlude is essentially a recap of the intro on Clapton's part, but Low dresses it up with his earlier 4ths fill over F♯m in measure 20 and a second-position fill that's framed off that open A chord. Barre your index finger at the 2nd fret, hammer onto fret 4 on strings 4 and 3 with your ring finger, and use your middle finger for the hammer-pull move on string 2.

## Bridge

The bridge modulates to the key of the G major, and both guitarists play similar patterns through the new descending chord progression. Here are the basic voicings Clapton uses through measure 30:

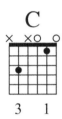   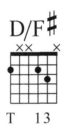  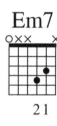

Notice that Clapton is using more of an arpeggio pattern here, generally speaking, than the verses, which were more block-chord style. But he's not terribly strict with any one pattern, so don't spend too much time trying to duplicate it exactly. It's better to find a pattern that feels and sounds good to you, as Clapton would probably not play it exactly the same twice anyway.

Measure 31 transitions back into the key of A major by way of an E–F♯m–E7/G♯ chord progression. This is similar to the rising dyads on strings 3 and 2 in measure 12 of the verse, but the difference here is that Clapton also walks up the bass note on string 6 along with it. Finger the E chord as normal (with middle, ring, and index), and then try middle/ring/pinky (low to high) for the F♯m and middle/ring/index for E7/G♯. This will allow you to leave the middle and ring fingers on the same strings for both chords.

## Guitar Solo

Clapton plays essentially the verse rhythm underneath the solo, which is played by Andy Fairweather Low. Low keeps things sparse and tasty here, paraphrasing the vocal melody with two approaches: single notes at first (for the "Would you know my name" line) and 6ths on strings 3 and 1 for the consequent phrase ("if I saw you in heaven?").

The single-note line (measures 32 and 36) begins in ninth position with your index and middle for the hammer-pull move. You'll need to briefly shift positions during the next phrase, but the tempo is slow enough that it's not difficult. For the 6ths line in measures 34–35 and 38–39, begin with your middle on string 3 and your index on string 1. For all the rest, keep your middle finger on string 3, using either your index or ring finger depending on whether the note on string 1 lies on the same fret (ring) or one below (index).

# TEARS IN HEAVEN
### Words and Music by Eric Clapton and Will Jennings

Tears in Heaven
Full Song

Intro
Slowly ♩ = 80

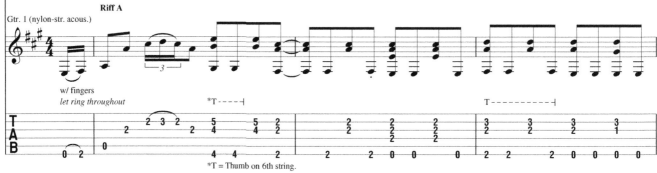

*T = Thumb on 6th string.

1., 4. Would you know my name _____ if I saw you in heav -
2. Would you hold my hand _____ if I saw you in heav -

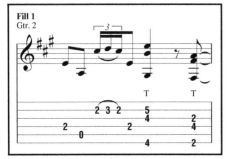 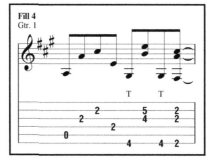 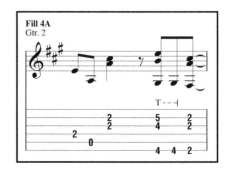

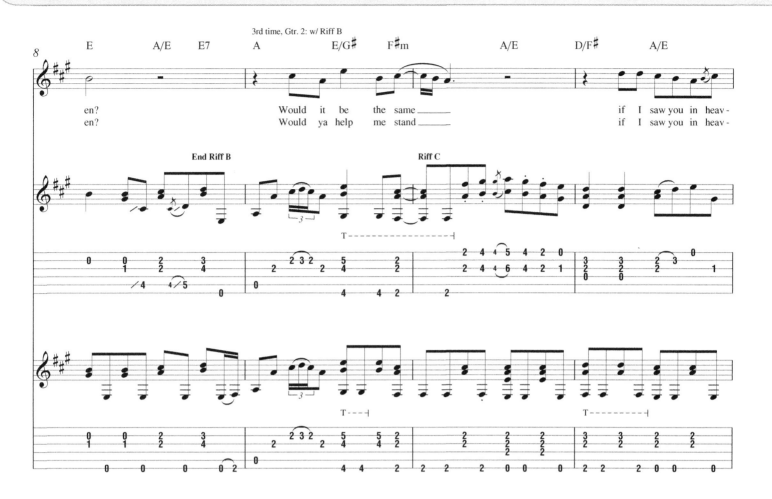

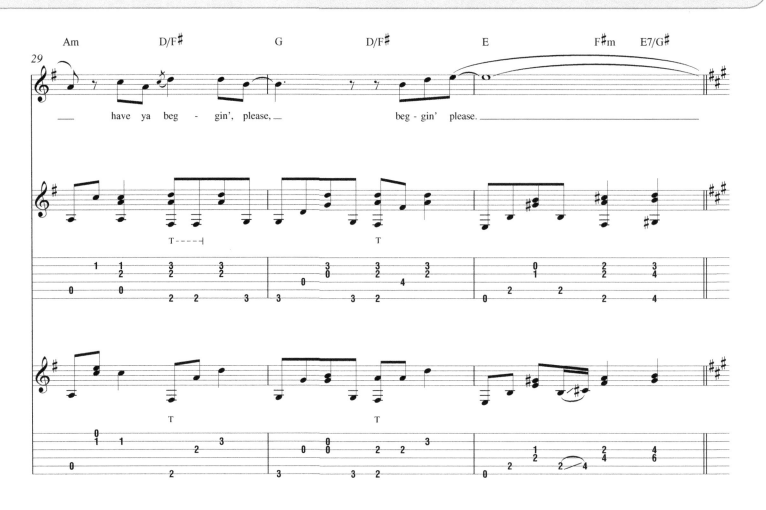

have ya beg - gin', please, _____                    beg - gin' please. _____

**Guitar Solo**

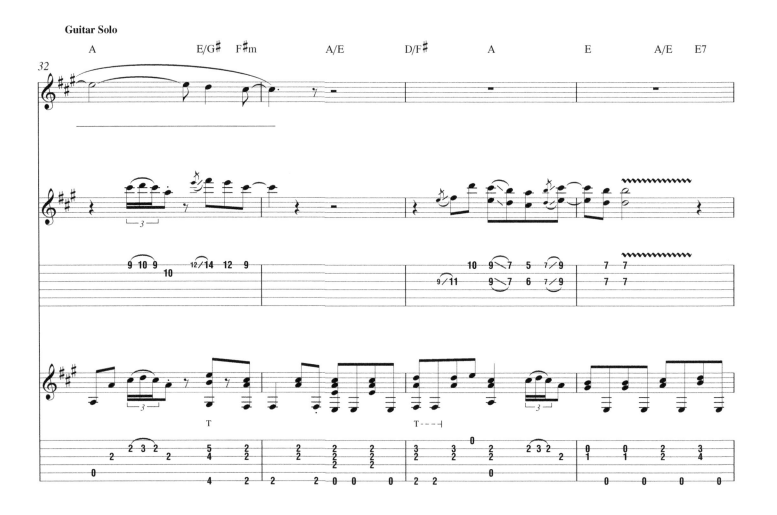

know      I   don't    be - long ___          here _ in  heav - en.

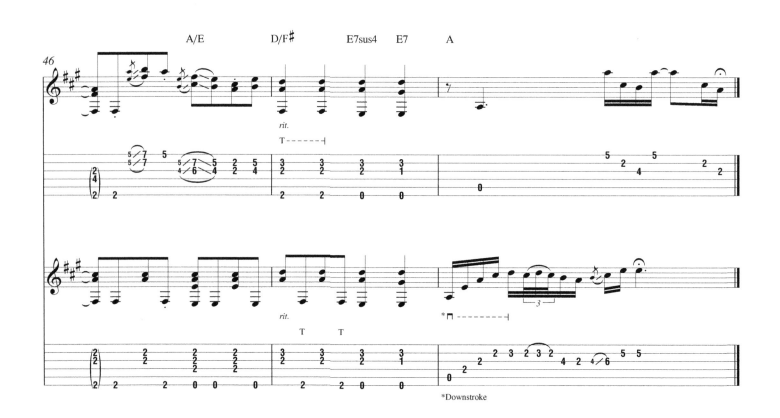

*Downstroke

# ESSENTIAL LICKS

This is the fun part of the book—nothing but licks! In this chapter, we'll take a look at countless licks in the style of Slowhand himself along with important nuggets about how to play them and/or what makes them tick. Many of these licks can be used in more than one setting—fast or slow, shuffle or straight, dominant or minor, etc.—so be sure to try them out in various contexts.

Like many blues players, Clapton often sticks with one scale throughout most of his solo, or at least for a good chunk of it. So we're going to break up this chapter by scale type. However, we'll also take a look at some licks that demonstrate how he can skillfully combine two scales at once, as well as make use of other melodic concepts.

## Minor Pentatonic Scale

First off is the good ol' minor pentatonic. Like most blues players, Eric spends the majority of his time mining this time-tested territory during his solo outings. For a scale containing only five notes, the amount of diversity that's achieved from player to player is astounding. Albert King's phrases sound completely different than B.B. King's, for example, and Clapton has certainly left his mark on this trusty melodic workhorse as well.

It should be noted that some of these licks could technically be labeled as blues scale licks because of the fact that the 4th degree will sometimes be bent a half step up to the "blue note," which is labeled as either the #4th or ♭5th. Some people even use the name "blues scale" to describe the minor pentatonic scale.

### Box 1

Let's start with some licks based out of the classic minor pentatonic box that almost every guitarist knows. In the key of G, it would appear in third position and look like this. The optional "blue notes" (which would technically turn this minor pentatonic scale into a blues scale) are indicated here with grey dots.

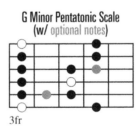

G Minor Pentatonic Scale
(w/ optional notes)

3fr

### Lick 1

This first lick in G is a three-measure phrase that works out the middle strings of this scale form. It would normally be played in a moderate-to-uptempo shuffle tune and is fairly active from start to finish. Don't miss the subtleties here that give the lick some added life, including the slide into the first note, the quarter-step bend on string 3, and the vibrato on the longest note in the example, which still only lasts a dotted quarter note. This lick can be played entirely with your first and third fingers.

Lick 1

## Lick 2

Here's another one in G that's in a similar vein to Lick 1. This one is a little more sophisticated, melodically, as we have some 4th intervals, which help to break things up a bit. This occurs at the spots where two consecutive 5th-fret notes occur on adjacent strings. With regards to fret-hand fingering for these, you have two options. You can play both with your third finger by fretting the first note (on the higher string) with the fleshier part and "rolling" over to the lower string. This requires some practice to make it sound smooth and avoid extraneous noises. Alternatively, you could fret the higher string with your third finger and, angling your hand, use your middle finger for the lower string. This method is generally easier to perform more cleanly, but experiment with both methods to see what suits you best. Also of note in this lick is the half-step bend from the minor to the major 3rd, which is a classic blues move.

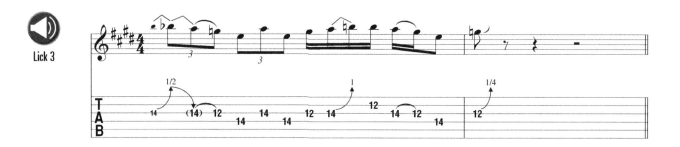

## Lick 3

Here's a lick in E, which moves us up to 12th position. This one demonstrates a bit more of the rock-tinged blues sound that Clapton and fellow guitar God Hendrix were perfecting during the late '60s. Notice the mixed rhythms, including triplets and 16th notes, and the bluesy half-step bend at the beginning. This lick can again be comfortably performed entirely with the first and third fingers, but beat 2 of measure 1 bears a little attention. After fretting the 14th fret on string 4, simply roll your finger over to string 3, using the pad of the finger to play string 3. With practice, you'll be able to get both notes clean with no bleeding of sound between them.

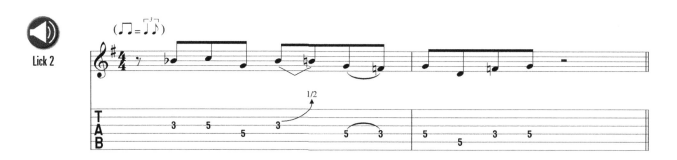

## Lick 4

Here's a 12/8 slow blues lick in C played in eighth position. Notice the repeated pull-off move on string 2, which Clapton will often repeat even more at increased tempos. In beat 3, we also see the same third-finger rolling move from string 4 to string 3 that we saw in Lick 3. Landing on the 5th (G) on string 5 creates a bold sound, which is heightened by the application of generous vibrato. Again, you can either roll your third finger from the note on string 4 immediately preceding this G note, or you can fret string 4 with your third finger and angle your hand to catch string 5 with your second finger.

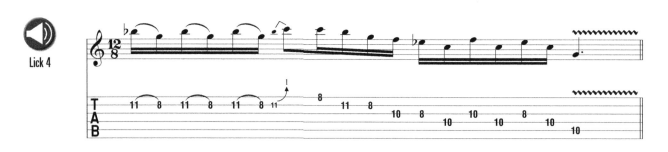

## Lick 5

This lick in D, which takes place in 10th position, contains one of Clapton's favorite devices in blues playing: the alteration of the root (D) with the *major* 7th (C♯). In this lick, this is achieved by pre-bending the 13th fret on string 2 up a whole step and releasing it only a half step. At that point, you'll need to stop the string from vibrating with your pick hand. This can be accomplished with either the pick or the palm. After stopping the string, immediately pre-bend the full whole step and pick the string, again releasing it only a half step. This move will take a little practice to sound as smooth as Clapton, but it's quite a striking sound when done properly.

## Lick 6

Here's another one in E that Clapton might play in a moderate straight-eighth groove. The double stops (two notes played at the same time) sound exceptionally thick and muscular and should be performed by partially barring your first finger. Finish off the lick by applying a strong vibrato on the root note (E) with your third finger.

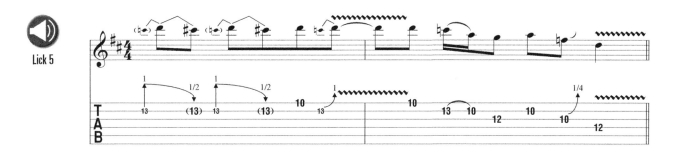

## Lick 7

In the same vein as Lick 6, this is one of Clapton's favorite devices in a moderate blues rock groove. There are only two notes at play here, but the rhythm is what gives the lick life. Play the E on string 1, play the D on string 2, and then bend the D up a whole step to E. All three of those moves occupy an equal amount of rhythmic time: i.e., they're each one 16th note long. So when you repeat that sequence over and over, you're playing a grouping of three 16th notes against a 4/4 beat. The short story is that it sounds really cool. And even though Clapton would bend the 15th fret with his ring finger only (with no support behind it), it's best to use your second finger behind your ring finger for added strength.

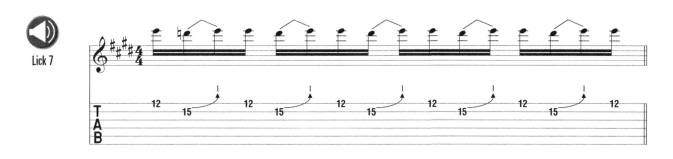

## Lick 8

Here's a lick in A that really cooks. It would fit nicely over an uptempo, straight-eighths blues rock groove. This is also a good lesson for readers of tab only. If you don't check out the notation, you'll be missing a very important part of this lick. See those little dots over the A and G notes in beat 2 of measure 1? Those are *staccato* markings, and they tell you to play those notes in a short, clipped manner. Try playing the lick with and without the staccato feel on those two notes, and you'll begin to understand how subtlety can make a huge difference in the feel of a phrase.

The A and G notes also present a bit of a fingering situation. If you can grab the G note on string 2 with your pinky, then you can handle the rest of the lick with fingers 1 and 3. But if you don't like to show the pinky love, then you might be forced to bend the note that follows (the D on beat 3) with your second finger. This is the way that Clapton would most likely do it, but that's still no reason to diss the pinky! Also check out the quick hammer-pull 16th-note triplet move at the beginning of measure 2—another Clapton favorite.

## Lick 9

Here's another one in the same uptempo vein of Lick 8. This one's also in A, but it takes place an octave higher in 17th position. It kicks off with a repetitive pull-off lick that builds great momentum and tension. This tension is released at the end of measure 1 with a whole-step bend up to the tonic A note, which is treated to some glorious vibrato, before we descend down the scale again with a rapid 16th-note line. Clapton would handle the notes in measure 1 with the third, first, and second fingers, catching the bend with the ring finger. Considering the cramped quarters at this region of the fretboard, this is most likely the preferred method for even the most ardent pinky-user.

To apply vibrato to a bent note, first bend the note to pitch and then slightly release and re-bend it over and over. It'll take practice to get a smooth sound, but it's a very musical sound when mastered, as Clapton so often demonstrates.

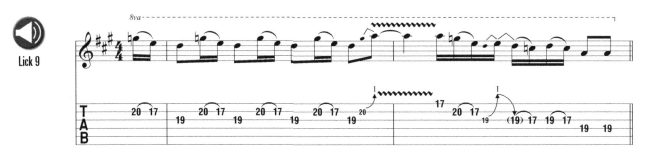

## Lick 10

Here's another rock-tinged one in D that touches on a few classic Clapton ideas. The first is the jump from string 1 to string 3 in beat 2 of measure 1. This leap helps to break it up melodically and prevents things from sounding too predictable. This is followed by a resolution to the low 5th (A in this case) on string 5 at the end of the measure. Again, you may want to fret this note with the middle finger to avoid having to roll the third finger.

In measure 2, we find the favorite Clapton move of hammering double stops in ascending groups of strings. This type of thing depends on which scale form you're working out of, but in this case, the same move could be transferred up one more string set as well (strings 3 and 2). Though the intervals would be different, it's still a great sound that Clapton uses often.

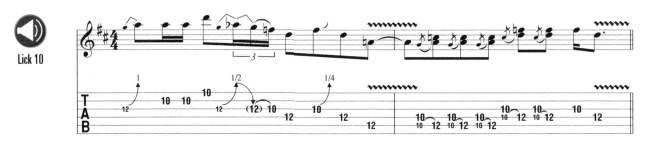

## Extension Box

And now let's check out a few licks from the upper extension box, which is sometimes named the "Albert King" box because many players cop his licks in this position. In reality, this is a bit of a misnomer, because Albert did not often play in this position at all. Instead he achieved the same licks by overbending notes fretted in the standard minor pentatonic box. At any rate, the extension position has been the framework for countless players' licks for decades; let's take a look at some in the style of Slowhand.

In case you're not familiar with this scale form, here it is in the key of G. This puts us in sixth position. Notice that the tonic of the scale (G, in this case) is located on string 2 and is indicated with the open circle. Again, the blue notes (the ♭5th) are indicated with grey dots.

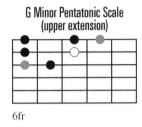

## Lick 11

Here's a rock lick in the key of D using this shape, which puts us in 13th position. After bending and holding the 15th-fret note (with the ring finger and middle behind it for support) on string 1 the second time, pick the string, quickly release the bend, and pull off to fret 13 for the 16th-note triplet. Immediately after pulling off, though, you'll need to bend a whole step again on fret 15 before finishing off the lick with a classic move used by everyone from Hendrix and Stevie Ray to rockers like Joe Satriani. Make the vibrato on the final note just about as intense as you can make it.

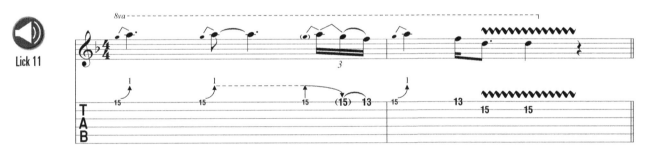

## Lick 12

This one is in D too and is another example of the three-over-four rhythmic idea we saw in Lick 7. Here, however, it's achieved with normally fretted notes and a hammer-on. The three-note fragment of C–D–F is repeated in even 16th notes for a full measure before resolving back on the tonic D note in measure 2. Notice that the three-note pattern takes three full beats before it cycles back around again. In other words, the series begins on C for beat 1, and it doesn't do that again until beat 4. It takes a little practice at first with this type of idea to keep your place rhythmically, so you don't lose your place in the measure.

Technically speaking, some people always play this idea with a partial barre of the first finger on fret 13. However, this results in the notes ringing together. If that's the desired effect, fine, but if you want the notes to sound distinct, as Clapton often does with this type of lick, you'll need to roll the first finger back and forth from string 2 to 1 in order to achieve the separation.

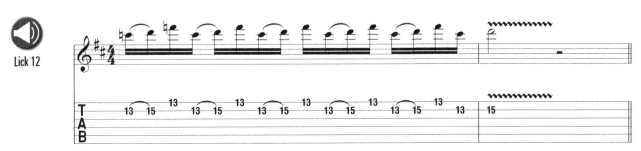

## Lick 13

Here's a slow blues lick in C that takes place in 11th position and demonstrates Clapton's intense side. Aside from beat 2, everything can be nicely handled with fingers 1 and 3. For beat 2, however, you'll need to fret the C note (fret 13) on string 2 with your second finger so that you can quickly follow it with your third finger on string 1 for the bend. Really dig in on this one and use plenty of attitude.

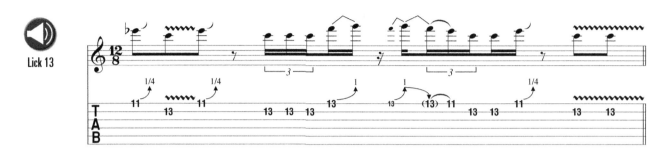

## Lick 14

The extension position is also constantly used in conjunction with the standard box position. Here's a good example of a classic move in this regard: sliding up from the ♭7th note on string 2 to the tonic. This one's in G, so we start off in third position. Use the third finger for the slide on string 2, which will put you in perfect position for the extended box form at sixth position. Don't miss the staccato marks at the beginning of measure 2. After barring with your first finger for the double stop at the 6th fret (beat 3.5), use either your second or third finger for the quick descending slide from fret 7 to 5 on the third string and finish it off with your first finger on the 3rd fret. This type of effortless traversing between scale forms is commonplace among the greats.

## Lick 15

Here's a similar idea in the key of A. This time, we're starting in the extended box, which puts us in eighth position. After some double-stop hammer-on moves on strings 1 and 2, we use the same descending slide move we used in Lick 14 to transition back down to the standard box 1 position.

# Major Pentatonic Scale

The major pentatonic is the brighter, twangier-sounding cousin of the minor pentatonic. You'll hear Eric make good use of this scale as well in both blues and rock. However, he doesn't often stick with this scale for an entire solo. He'll usually combine major pentatonic phrases with minor pentatonic ones to broaden his sonic color palette. For now, though, let's take a look at some of his favorite major pentatonic ideas.

## Box 1

Clapton doesn't often make use of this entire scale form in his soloing; he tends to stick to the higher strings. But here's box 1 of the major pentatonic scale form in the key of G, which puts us in the second or third position.

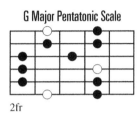

G Major Pentatonic Scale

2fr

## Lick 16

This lick in A takes place in fifth position and would sound good on an uptempo straight-eighth groove. The beginning is easily played with your first and third fingers; use a first-finger barre for the double stop at the 5th fret. For the bluesy hammer-on from C to C# on string 3, use your first and second fingers, respectively, and finish off with your third finger for the final A note on string 4.

## Lick 17

This lick is full of spirit. It's also in A, but it's an octave higher, which puts us way up in 17th position. Make those whole-step bends in the beginning crisp and clean, using the middle finger behind the ring for support. For the vibrato on the A notes with your first finger, you're going to need to slightly bend the string up toward the ceiling and release repeatedly; any other movement would result in the string sliding off the fretboard. The 16th-16th-8th rhythm on beats 2 and 3 of measure 2 really gooses this lick in terms of momentum, and this is the type of motif that could be extended for much longer if the mood strikes.

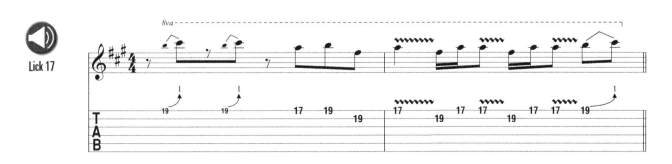

## Lick 18

This one is in the key of G in the upper octave, which puts us in 15th position. It's kind of the major pentatonic version of Lick 12, and we're using that same group-of-three idea in straight 16th notes. In this one, though, we answer the ascending lick of the first measure with a descending version of the lick in measure 2. Measure 1 could be fretted with either your first and third or first and second fingers (due to the cramped space), but measure 2 is probably best handled the way Clapton would do it: ring-index-middle, ring-index-middle, etc.

## Lick 19

This one is in the key of E and is actually played in open position. It's a classic country blues lick that's found its way into countless solos over the years. Regarding the open E string, this lick will sound equally nice whether you let it ring out or not, so try it both ways and see which one suits your fancy.

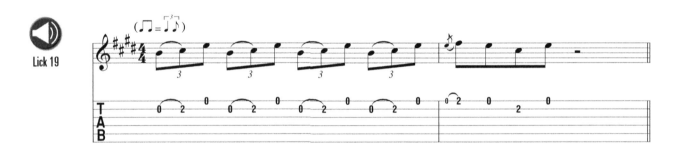

## Lick 20

Here's another one in E, except we're an octave higher in 11th and 12th position. Notice how it's essentially just climbing the scale, but the rhythm helps frame it into a nice little lick. The syncopated (stressing the off-beat) double stop at the end gives it a nice little lift and helps the resolution stand out a bit. It's recommended that you use your middle finger for the slide from F♯ to G♯ on string 3, as this will put you in 12th position, which is exactly where you need to be to finish it up.

Regarding the vibrato on the final double stop, this will take a bit of practice. You'll be adding vibrato to a barred finger, which will probably feel a little unusual at first, so take your time with it. Again, you won't be able to pull the string down toward the floor, or you'll slide off the fretboard, so all the motion will need to be toward the ceiling.

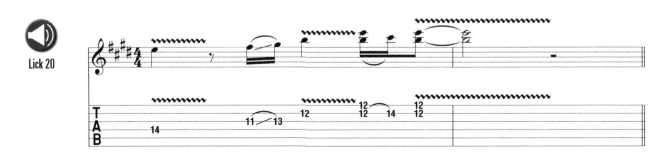

## Box 3

This is Clapton's preferred scale form for the major pentatonic scale, although he tends to stay on the top three strings mostly when using it. It puts the tonic note on string 2, which is usually fretted with the index finger, though the middle finger may also be used in certain situations. In the key of G, this puts us in seventh or eighth position.

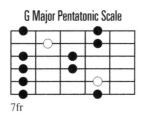

G Major Pentatonic Scale

## Lick 21

Here's one from this form in the key of D, which puts us up in 15th position. You'll no doubt recognize this one as a southern rock favorite, as it's been adopted whole-heartedly by the genre. Begin by giving the E note just a slight bluesy bend with the ring finger and continue with your index finger for D and your middle finger for the B note on string 3. The real payoff of this lick happens next, though. While bending string 2 up a whole step at fret 17 and holding it there with the ring finger (supported with the middle behind it), use your pinky for fret 17 on string 1. After that, pick the still bent second string and release it.

While this fingering is common, some players that don't often use the pinky (such as Clapton), will bend the second string with the middle finger and fret the first string with the ring finger. Feel free to try both and see which suits you best. At this part of the neck, the frets are fairly close, which makes the middle-and-ring combination easy. At lower regions of the fretboard, however, it may prove to be more troublesome.

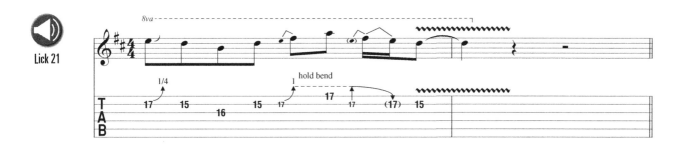

## Lick 22

This one's also in D from the same position. Plant the first finger on the 15th fret of string 2 and sting it with vibrato every time you hit it. The middle finger can handle all the B notes on string 3, and you can use your ring finger for the final bend. If this one sounds familiar, there's good reason: take a look back at Lick 17. Measure 2 of that lick is essentially the same thing transposed to the key of A and using the Box 1 form! The lesson to be learned here is that you should know how to play the same lick in multiple positions on the fretboard.

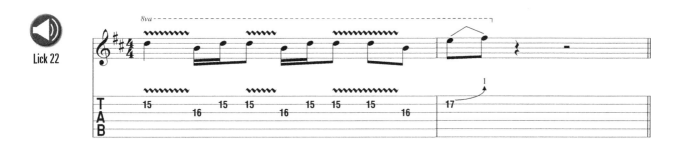

## Lick 23

Here's a slow, soulful lick in the key of C, which takes place in 13th position. After bending the 15th fret a whole step to E and adding some lyrical vibrato, we quickly peck out the 13th-fret C note and immediately answer it with a soaring whole-step bend on the first string, which is eventually released just before the end of the measure. To cap it off, we bend and release fret 15 on string 2 and resolve to the tonic C note at fret 13, again adding vibrato—this time with the first finger. This lick can be handled entirely with the index and ring finger for frets 13 and 15, respectively.

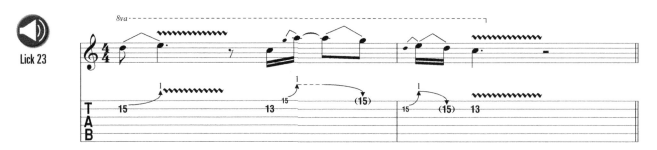

## Lick 24

In the same vein as Lick 23, this one's in C and is all about the string bending. After an ascending run up through the middle strings, which should be fingered in 12th position, with the middle finger catching the C note on string 2, we launch into an incredibly lyrical phrase that will test your bending abilities. After picking the 15th fret at the beginning of the measure, you execute a series of repeated eighth-note whole-step bends and releases in time across three and a half beats before resolving with the C–D–C notes at the end. Depending on your tone, and the amount of resulting sustain, this lick can sound quite different, so feel free to try it clean, slightly distorted, and fully fuzzed out to hear the possibilities.

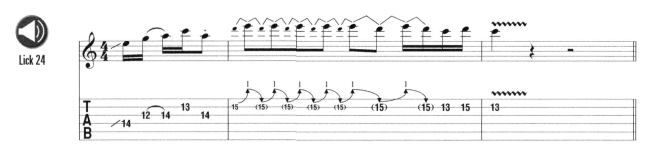

## Lick 25

We're back in the key of D here in 15th position for this one. It begins with a similar move that's found in Lick 21, with a whole-step bend on the 17th fret of string 2 followed by the 17th fret on string 1. That's where the similarities end, though, because you'll need to follow that with the D note on string 2 with your first finger and the B on string 3 with your middle. As with Lick 21, you can choose to bend that 17th-fret note (E) with your middle or ring finger, which necessitates either the ring or pinky, respectively, for the high A note on string 1.

Apply a good bit of vibrato to the D note on beat 3 with the index finger. The move on beat 3 may prove a bit troublesome at first, because it's a bit unexpected. After fretting the B on string 3 with your middle finger, you'll need to immediately jump up to string 1 and bend the 17th-fret A note up a soaring whole step and release it before finally resolving to the tonic D note on string 2, again applying vibrato with the index finger. The leap from string 3 to string 1 for the bend wouldn't be as troublesome if you were fretting with the first finger on string 3, but since you're using the middle finger for the B note, you won't have much time to get the middle finger lined up behind the ring to support the bend. Because of this, it may be necessary to clip that B note on string 3 short just a little bit. Since the high bend is the clear climax of this lick, the effect will be negligible.

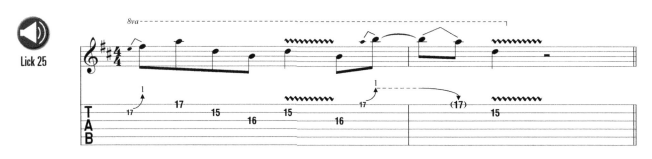

# Composite Blues Scale

The "composite blues scale" is a name often used to describe the combination of the major pentatonic scale and the blues scale. Clapton is especially adept at this type of scale combination, and we'll take a look here at some of his typical licks in this scale.

## Box 1

Box 1 of this scale in the key of G would put us in second and third position and would look like this:

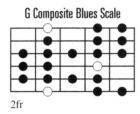

It's important to note that Clapton (or most players for that matter) doesn't usually play all of these notes in ascending or descending fashion as a "scale" per se—the way one may play straight up or down a minor pentatonic scale for a bit, for instance—but they're all available from which to choose at any given time.

### Lick 26

This lick in E demonstrates one of the most classic uses of this scale in a blues shuffle. We're in 12th position here, and this one would fit perfectly over bars 11–12 of a 12-bar—also known as the *turnaround*. If you look closely, the only note here that comes from the major pentatonic scale is the G# note (fret 13 on string 3), but it makes all the difference.

If you're a pinky user, you can easily assign one finger per fret to this line all throughout measure 1. In measure 2, however, you may want to fret the final low B note on string 5 with your second finger, which will prevent you from having to roll the third finger.

### Lick 27

This one's in the key of G and would sound good over a straight-eighth blues rock groove. Another classic scale-combining device, this idea mimics a well-known organ lick and can be played comfortably in third position. After the grace-note hammered dyad on frets 3 and 4 of strings 3 and 2, we have the 5th-fret dyad. Most players tend to grab this by simply flattening out the ring finger into a partial barre, although you could instead use your ring and pinky finger if you choose.

On beat 4 of measure 1, we have another neat trick: the double-stop trill. Barre your first finger to cover fret 3 on strings 3 and 2 and then quickly hammer and pull to and from the 4th fret with your middle finger. The overall effect should be the sound of B and D with a slight fluctuation. It'll take a little practice to work the trill up to speed, so don't be discouraged if yours doesn't sound really smooth at first.

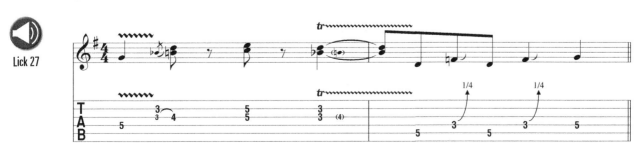

## Lick 28

Here's another one in the same vein as Lick 27. In beat 3 of measure 1, we have a pre-bend and release. After playing the 3rd and 5th fret on string 2 with your index and ring finger, respectively, you'll need to quickly and silently bend the second string a half step. You then pick the bent string and release it. You shouldn't hear any ascending of pitch at all; then only thing you should hear is an F note bending down to the E note.

In measure 2, we see the one-string version of the double-stop trill we had in Lick 27. This simply omits the second string, which should make it a bit easier. This whole lick lays out perfectly in third position and, save for the trill (which should be performed with your index and middle fingers), can all be handled with your index and ring fingers.

## Lick 29

This lick is in the key of D and takes us to 10th position. It includes some of Eric's most tasteful scale-mixing ideas. After beginning with the tonic D note on string 4 with your ring finger, quickly shift back to grab the 10th fret on string 3 with your middle finger and slide quickly and smoothly up to fret 11. This will put you in an advantageous position for the moves to follow. The D and A notes on strings 1 and 2, respectively, at fret 10 should be handled by rolling your index finger—not barring—as we don't want the notes to bleed together. In order to do this, you'll need to plan ahead just a bit and fret string 1 with more of the pad of the finger rather than the tip. This will allow you to roll over to the tip for the note on string 2.

Continue on by pre-bending the 12th fret on string 1 with your third finger (backed up by the middle) up a half step, pick it, and then release it, resolving the first half of the phrase with the tonic D note at fret 10 on string 1, treated to some vibrato with the index finger. At the beginning of measure 2, most players will tend to grab the B note at fret 12 on string 2 with their second finger, which will enable them to use their ring finger for the impressive bending maneuvers that follow. After first bending fret 13 up a whole step, you'll need to alternate pre-bending between a whole step and a half step in an eighth-note rhythm. This isn't quite as easy as Clapton can make this type of thing sound, so work slowly at first and be sure your intonation (tuning) is good on the bends. It's a good idea to check your pitch against the unbent notes (string 1 at frets 15 and 14, respectively, in this case) at first to be sure you're on the mark.

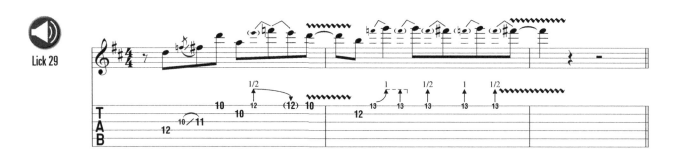

## Lick 30

Here's a lick in A that takes us all the way up to the stratospheric 17th position. This one again features some nifty bending, as it begins with a whole-step bend at fret 20 followed immediately by a half-step bend on the same fret. The targeted notes here are the 4th (D) and the major 3rd (C#), and since they're both being bent from the minor 3rd (C), the effect is nice and bluesy. You can hear Angus Young cop this type of thing in his solo from "You Shook Me All Night Long" (key of G instead of A).

After bending the 20th fret on string 2 up a whole step and adding a good dose of vibrato, we careen down what appears to be a minor pentatonic run, only to be surprised at the end when the line resolves to C# (the major 3rd) at fret 18. Regarding the left hand, most players would handle all the 20th- and 19th-fret notes with the ring finger, the 17th-fret notes with the index, and the 18th fret at the end with the middle. Again, accuracy of pitch on the bends is important, so check against unbent pitches at first if necessary.

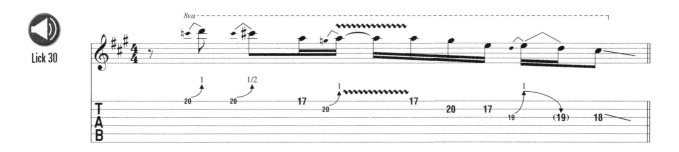

## Lick 31

This lick in A could be thought of as the straight-eighth blues rock version of the blues shuffle idea in Lick 26. We're in fifth position here, and again, the only note not found in the minor pentatonic scale is the major 3rd—C# in this case. But it colors the entire lick. After stinging the first note on string 4 with some ring-finger vibrato, we have a quick 16th-note run that kicks off with a hammer-on from fret 5 to 6 on string 3. Immediately after this move, you can use a partial barre with your index finger for the 5th-fret notes that follow on strings 2 and 1, respectively. You can try rolling your index finger to make the notes distinct, but at faster tempos, such as the one in which this lick is typically played, the difference between the two methods is fairly negligible.

Clapton would most likely use his ring finger for the 8th fret on string 2 on beat 3, but why don't you give the pinky a try and see how that feels? By doing that, you won't need to alter your hand position at all. At the end of measure 1, use a partial barre with your index finger for the 5th-fret notes and then hammer to fret 6 with your middle finger. The ending of this lick, with the two E notes appearing at octaves apart, is a classic turnaround move that you'll find in countless songs. This entire lick would most likely be heard in measures 11–12 of a 12-bar blues form in A.

## Lick 32

This is another uptempo lick in A that takes place in the higher octave at 17th position. You shouldn't need to veer from a one-finger-per-fret approach at all for this one. After kicking it off with a vibratoed tonic note on string 4, we see a nifty device called a *pedal point*. This is a phrase in which different notes are alternated with the same note over and over. In this case, fret 17 on string 2 (the E note), is our pedal point, and we alternate third-string C♯ and D notes with it on frets 18 and 19, respectively. Also note the "bouncy" rhythm of a dotted 8th and 16th used here, which helps to draw less attention to the pedal point than usual, since it's given a shorter duration than the other notes. After this major-sounding phrase, we quickly shift gears in measure 2 with a minor pentatonic phrase to finish it off.

Lick 32

## B.B. Box

The "B.B. Box" is a name given to a scale form fragment on the top three strings. Named for its heavy use by the King himself, Clapton has, along with almost every warm-blooded blues player, made extensive use of this form as well. It's a composite scale in a sense that it's common for players to pluck several different notes from its fret "branches," as it were. Let's take a look at one representation of this scale form in the key of G, which places the tonic G note on string 2 and puts us mostly in eighth position.

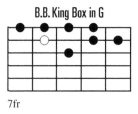

B.B. King Box in G

7fr

The B note at fret 7 on string 1 lies technically outside the "box shape," but it is included at times in licks largely derived from this shape, so I've included it here. Also, the "blue note"—in this case, C♯ or D♭ at fret 9 on string 1—is also kind of optional, but it does see a decent bit of action as well.

If you look closely, you may recognize many of these notes from the Box 3 form of the major pentatonic scale. And you'd be correct; this is the same positioning. The difference is that the B.B. box also includes notes from the composite scale.

## Lick 33

Here's a lick in E that sounds great over a blues shuffle. You can remain in fifth position throughout here with a one-finger-per-fret approach. To start, silently pre-bend the 7th fret on string 2 up a half step. Pick the note, release the bend, and then pull off to the 5th fret, which is fretted by your index finger. Next is a nifty little move that typifies the B.B. box. The sound of the 2nd (F♯) moving down to the 6th (C♯) and resolving to the tonic (E) is just a great sound that you'll hear over and over again from players in this position. Give that E note some vibrato with the index finger, and then end the first part of the phrase with a clipped half-step bend on the 7th fret of string 2 again.

Measure 2 displays a great device that's often used by Clapton and many other great soloists: the *theme and variation*. Notice how measure 2 begins similarly to measure 1, but it's not quite the same. The rhythms are a little different, and the phrase is more succinct, which provides a nice bookend to the larger two-bar structure.

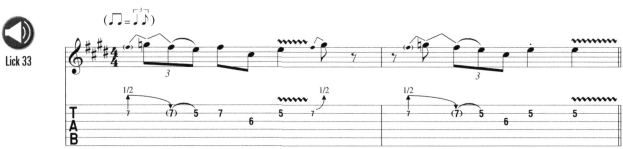

Lick 33

## Lick 34

This one is in D and puts us in 15th position. We're only using three notes here: D, B, and F. Be careful with the rhythms in this one; there are some eighths where you may expect 16ths and vice versa. Notice also the repetitive three-note grouping of 16th notes that briefly takes hold beginning on beat 2.5.

If you're a pinky player, you can handle the 18th fret with your pinky. Clapton, however, as well as many other blues players, would use his third finger. Whichever you choose, make sure the 16th notes are steady and even. For the final two notes, just continue adding vibrato as if you were playing a half note. The only difference is that you'll pick again on beat 2.

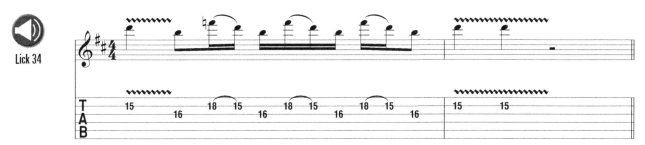

## Lick 35

This one in C really shows off the frame of the B.B. box beautifully. We're in 13th position here, and we begin with an attention-getting line containing some wide leaps. The rhythm is also noteworthy here, as the broken triplet line of beat 1 really gooses the momentum. The theme and variation idea we talked about in Lick 33 returns here as well. Notice how the same three-note phrase, A–C–G, is used in measure 2 as a launching pad for an extended, flashier phrase that concludes with a quick hammer-pull move—one of Clapton's favorite devices. Listen for this type of idea in a moderate to uptempo blues shuffle.

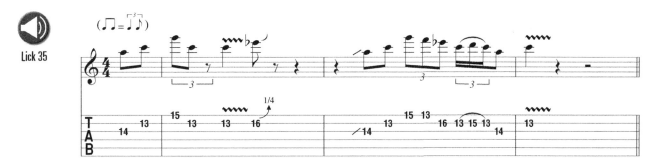

## Lick 36

Another one in C that works over the same blues shuffle groove as Lick 35, this one is all about being "in the cracks." After a brief pickup phrase (A–C), we squarely land on the E♭ note at fret 16 of string 2. This note is the minor 3rd in the key of C, and our target is the major 3rd, or E. This means we need to bend it a half step. The thing is that we just take our ever-loving sweet time getting there. Try to time it so that you reach the E note on beat 4 (or even later if you'd like). At measure 2, the tension is released with a minor pentatonic phrase. Notice, again, how the E♭ at fret 16 is teased with a bluesy quarter-step bend before the phrase comes to resolution by bending the E♭ quickly up a half step at the end of measure 2. Regarding the fret hand, most players, including Eric, would most likely use the ring finger for all the 16th-fret notes.

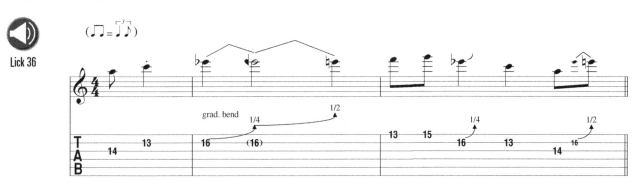

## Lick 37

Here's yet another similar one in C that demonstrates another of Clapton's tricks: the *overbend.* After riding on the vibrato-laden tonic at fret 13 on string 2, we bend the 16th-fret E♭ note not up a whole step, but up *two whole steps* to G. Depending on the gauge of your strings, this may prove to be quite difficult at first. Once you do finally reach your destination, slowly release the bend over the course of the next three beats before finishing off with the rapid-fire hammer-pull move. Though, again, Clapton bends without the support of his middle finger behind his ring, this is not recommended here unless you've been playing that way since the beginning!

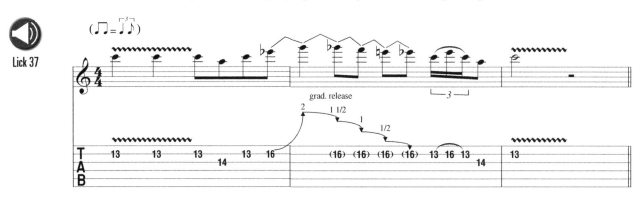

## Lick 38

We're in the key of A for this slow 12/8 lick in 10th position. After a classic pickup phrase involving the 6th (F♯) and tonic (A)—don't forget to slide up into the first note!—we play a nice, measured whole-step bend on fret 12 of string 2. You should reach your destination pitch shortly before you clip the note. Next up is another overbend like we saw in Lick 37. This time, however, we're only bending up 1-1/2 steps. This is something that B.B. does all the time, and many greats, including Slowhand, have borrowed this little trick. You could, of course, hit this same pitch by bending the 13th fret up a whole step, which is the more common way, but the sound is slightly different. Try it both ways to hear the difference. We close out with Clapton's patented hammer-pull riff and one staccato tonic A note before the final declaration on the downbeat of measure 2, which is treated to characteristic vibrato.

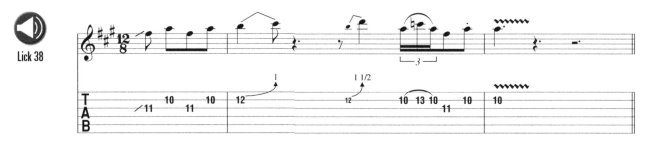

## Lick 39

This one takes place over a moderate to uptempo blues shuffle in E, which puts us in fifth position. While the melody here is certainly catchy, it's the rhythm that's the tricky part. We talked earlier about the three-over-four effect of repeating a group of three notes in a straight-16th rhythm. Well, that's kind of child's play compared to this. After the pickup, we start to play a descending triplet line—so far, so good. After five notes, however, we start to repeat it from the top. The problem—and the really cool thing about this—is that five notes don't neatly line up as triplets. So we have a five-note repeating phrase that's played as triplets. It's very easy to lose your place here, as this is not a grouping that most ears are accustomed to. The good news is that the phrase is only repeated once before the pattern is broken for the resolution. If it had been repeated even once more, it would increase the difficulty significantly. Due to the distance of the frets at this place on the neck, I'd advise using your pinky for fret 8 at the end of measure 1, even though Clapton would use his ring finger.

## Lick 40

Another blues shuffle lick, this one is in G at eighth position and milks a few devices for all they're worth. First off, notice the staccato mark in the pickup phrase; this minor detail makes quite a difference in the lick's setup. In particular, the soaring whole-step bend on fret 10 is made that much more dramatic when preceded by a bit of silence. On beat 2, we see the patented Clapton hammer-pull move, but here it's on string 1 and alternates between the 4th degree (C) and the ♭5th blues note for a particularly nasty effect. To contrast this, another hammer-pull move appears on beat 4 that makes use of the much more consonant tonic (G) and 2nd (A) notes.

You should definitely use your ring finger supported by the middle for the 10th-fret bend, but the fingering for the remainder of the lick is open for debate. Clapton would use his ring finger for all the 11th- and 10th-fret notes, but if you're a pinky player, it would come in mighty handy here for fret 11.

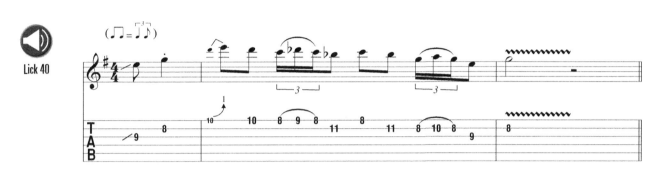

# ESSENTIAL RIFFS

From his days with the Bluesbreakers through his comeback in the late '80s, Clapton has graced us with some doozies in the riff department. In this chapter, we're going to look at ten of his most memorable. We'll examine them in detail, much like the five songs, and equip you with everything you need to know to pull them off the way Slowhand does. These will be arranged in chronological order.

## *"Sunshine of Your Love"*
### From *Disraeli Gears*, 1967

Coming off his stint with the Bluesbreakers, Clapton had conquered England. With the release of Cream's *Disraeli Gears* in 1967, the world was soon to follow. The biggest hit from the album, and basically Cream's signature song, "Sunshine of Your Love" contains *the* prototypical rock guitar riff.

The riff, which is doubled by Jack Bruce on bass guitar, begins in 10th position out of the D blues scale. While the typical blues scale box pattern remains in 10th position through all six strings, Clapton is using a lower extension as he travels to the lower register. Taken together, the scale form would look like this:

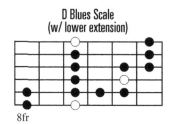

So, although he begins in 10th position, by the bottom of the phrase, he's shifted down to eighth. This riff isn't terribly difficult, but it just grooves like no one's business. Use all downstrokes with the pick and really dig in to get some bite to the tone. I'd suggest playing frets 12, 11, and 10 on string 5 in 10th position and then shifting down to eighth position for fret 10 on string 6. But the tempo is slow enough that shifting isn't really a concern.

After two times through the two-measure riff, Clapton adds some serious girth in measure 5 by harmonizing it with *open-voiced* triads. An open-voiced triad is one in which the notes span more than one octave. He begins with this D major chord form:

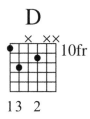

Since he's strumming these chords with a pick, you'll need to deaden the fourth string by touching it with your ring or middle finger, while the curvature of your index finger can lightly touch strings 1 and 2 to keep them quiet (see photo). This same form is moved down two frets for the C chord.

After the first four chordal strums, he resumes the riff in single notes as before, except for the end, where he moves up an octave for the D–F–D melody. Note also the use of the double stop at fret 12 on beat 2.5 of measure 6, and the triple stop in measure 8, for added thickness.

The last detail that needs to be mentioned is the glorious vibrato that Clapton adds to the F note at the end of each phrase. See the vibrato section in the Techniques chapter for more on Clapton's vibrato. Suffice it to say that this riff won't sound quite the same without it at those spots!

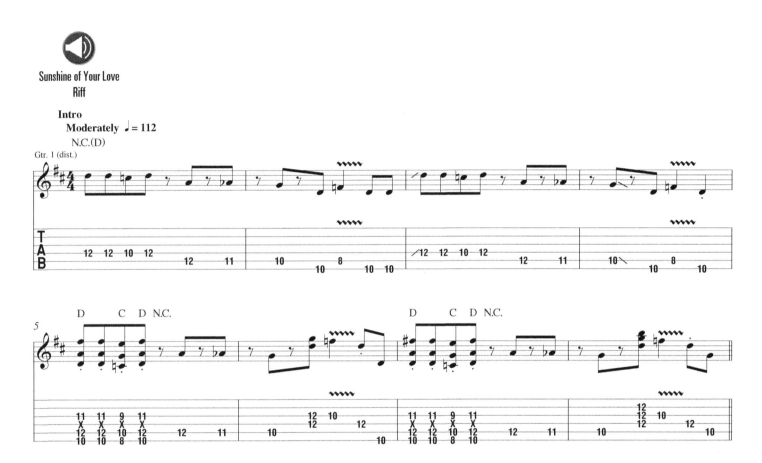

Sunshine of Your Love
Riff

# "White Room"
## From, *Wheels of Fire*, 1968

"White Room" is another one of Cream's most famous songs, and it too is replete with fantastic guitar work from Clapton. A hit from the *Wheels of Fire* album in 1968, the song contains a common chord position that's been used in some way by many bands throughout the days, including the Beatles, Blind Faith, and many more.

After the choral-sounding intro in the unusual time signature of 5/4, the verse kicks in, and Clapton rolls out the famous chord riff. The song is an excellent example of *modal mixture*, as some chords here are derived from the D major scale, and others the D minor scale. The chord progression of D–C5–G/B–B♭5–C5 is articulated by Clapton in mostly open position in a fairly non-syncopated fashion, though the dotted eighth/16th rhythm on beat 2 of measure 1 certainly adds a nice lift.

Notice that Clapton extends his first finger barre to the sixth string for the Bb5 and C5 power chords, creating a thicker sound. Clapton isn't terribly precise with his picking through each chord, so don't spend too much time trying to duplicate it exactly. Just work on getting the basic feel down (as depicted here), and feel free to add slight variations (as he does) when you see fit.

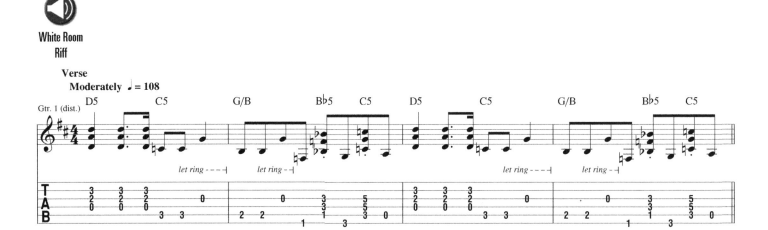

## "Let It Rain"
### From *Eric Clapton*, 1970

The year 1970 was a busy one for Clapton, as it saw the release of both his eponymous solo debut and *Layla and Other Assorted Love Songs* with Derek and the Dominos. *Eric Clapton* hit #13 on the strength of the two hit singles: "After Midnight" (#18) and "Let It Rain" (#48). Both have become classics in their own right, but the latter's intro riff packs a serious punch.

Clapton creates a mini guitar orchestra to usher in this song consisting of one acoustic rhythm guitar and three lead guitars in harmony. The chord progression is simple: A–G–G–A. And the acoustic (Gtr. 4) lays the foundation by strumming open-position voicings of those chords.

The lead guitars all harmonize in perfect three-part harmony with melodies that highlight the chords. Gtr. 1 begins on string 2 in third position with a ring-finger slide from fret 3 to 5. You can roll your index finger for the transition from measure 1 to 2 on the third-fret notes. In measure 3, begin with your index finger for the slide, as that will put you in good position for the remainder of the phrase. For the final note of measure 3—the A note at fret 5 on string 1—either use your pinky or slightly shift up to grab it with the ring finger. In measure 4, we have a syncopated line that can be handled comfortably in second position, though you'll have to roll your index finger from string 3 to 2 for the final two notes at the 2nd fret.

For Gtr. 2, begin with a ring-finger slide as well, and use the index and ring finger for all the notes until the end of measure 3, when the middle finger should fret the E note on string 2. Again, measure 4 can be handled in second position, though you'll be required to roll both the ring finger (for the 4th fret) and index finger (for the 2nd fret). Gtr. 3 should use the same exact fingering as Gtr. 2 through measure 3 (ring and index for all notes). For measure 4, however, you'll begin in fifth position, hammering from fret 5 to 7 on string 5 with the index and ring and taking fret 5 on string 4 with the index. At that point, you'll shift to fourth position, using the middle for fret 5, string 5 and the index for fret 4, string 4. Then you'll shift down once again to second position for the last two notes, taking them with the ring (string 5) and index (string 4).

Measures 5–7 are an exact repeat of 1–3. For Gtr. 1, measure 8 could be handled entirely in second position if you're a pinky user. If not, just shift to third position for the final two notes on string 2. For Gtr. 2, shift to second position, with your middle finger on fret 3, string 2, and the rest of it will fall in line easily. For Gtr. 3, shift to second position at the beginning of the measure, using your ring finger for fret 4, string 3.

**Let It Rain**
**Riff**

# *"Layla"*
## From *Layla and Other Assorted Love Songs*, 1970

If one were challenged with the immense task of picking Eric Clapton's signature song, "Layla" would certainly have to be a strong contender. Boasting one of the most recognizable riffs in all of rock, let alone Clapton's multi-decade career, it's been a staple of classic rock radio ever since it was eligible and will no doubt continue to be for the foreseeable future.

As with "Let It Rain," which came out the same year, "Layla" begins with another multi-layered guitar onslaught. Evidently, Clapton was in an orchestral mindset at this period. There are three guitars, but they are divided into two main parts. Gtrs. 1 & 2 each play the pentatonic single-note riff, an octave apart, and sustain the final note. Gtr. 3 also begins with the pentatonic riff, but it continues on with the main power chord riff on the lower strings.

Both Gtrs. 1 & 3 are working out of the open-position D minor pentatonic scale form for the single-note riff. The full form looks like this:

Gtr. 2, which is playing an octave higher than Gtrs. 1 & 3, is working out of seventh position and using this scale form of D minor pentatonic, which is sometimes referred to as form 5 (or box 5):

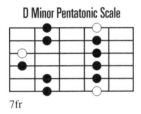

Though these riffs are a little speedy, they're not all that difficult, especially considering the legato moves used. The biggest challenge is making every note speak clearly and keeping the rhythm steady. It's very easy for hammer-pull moves to have a lopsided sound because of rushing. So it's important to start slowly and make sure that everything is clean and even before speeding up. For Gtrs. 1 & 3, you'll most likely want to use the ring finger for the 3rd-fret notes. For Gtr. 2, unless you're a real stickler for using the pinky, you'll probably go the Clapton route and use the index and ring.

For how effortless it sounds, the power chord riff of Gtr. 3 actually requires a little pre-planning. After the open D string on the downbeat, you'll need to shift to fifth position for the D5. You can either play this chord with the index and ring fingers or index and pinky. I prefer the pinky because it's a more natural fit for the larger frets, but choose whichever you feel most comfortable with. After picking the D5, slide down to C5 without picking, and then shift down and pick B♭5. This all happens fairly quickly, so you may have to start slowly to work it up.

Next, leaving your finger on string 4 (pinky or ring), take your index off string 5 to reveal the open A string for the A/F dyad. Next is the tricky part. You have two choices for the 3rd fret on string 6. You can:

- Shift your index finger to fret 3, string 6, and then simply move up one string for the C5 chord, or
- Play fret 3, string 6 with your middle finger and then shift up to third position for the C5.

If you do the latter, you can keep your pinky (or ring finger) on string 4, which is nice. For the next move, again remove your index, keeping the fourth string fretted, for the A/G dyad. Then use your index for fret 3, string 6 and quickly shift up for the final D5 chord. Phew!

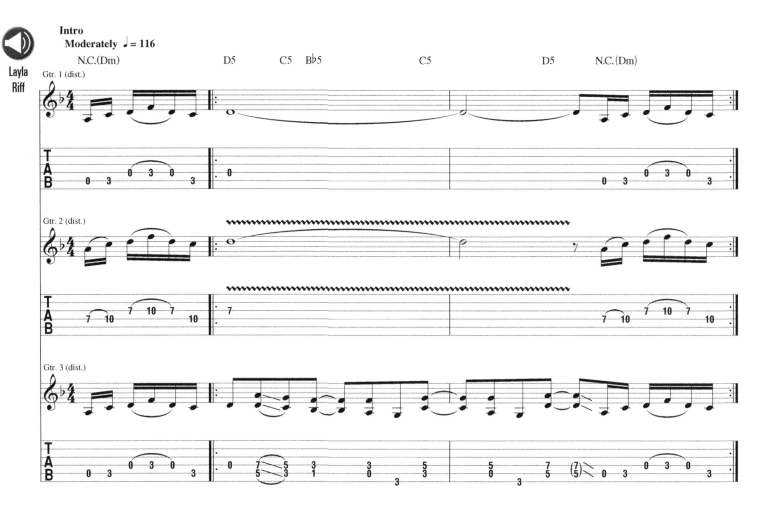

# "Cocaine"
## From *Slowhand*, 1977

One of the several J.J. Cale-written songs with which Clapton had a hit ("After Midnight" was another), "Cocaine" appeared on his 1977 *Slowhand* album and told a cautionary tale about the powerful drug. As far as riffs go, they don't get much simpler, but sometimes simplicity just does the trick.

The song opens with three guitar parts: Gtr. 3, which plays only chords, Gtr. 1, which begins playing chords and then moves to low-register fills, and Gtr. 2, which plays mid-register fills only. We have two chords here, people: E and D. That's rock 'n' roll. Gtr. 3 pounds out the A-form barre chords (see chords in transcription) in the syncopated rhythmic hook that drives the song, allowing the D chord to sustain the full span of measure 2.

Gtr. 1 begins in unison with Gtr. 3, but by the middle of measure 2, it abandons the chords for a more exciting life of fills. On beat 3 of measure 2, Clapton trills from the open fifth string to fret 2 using his middle finger. Trills aren't as easy as they sound at first, so don't be discouraged if it takes a while to build up the speed (and endurance). The concept is simple: hammer on from the open string to fret 2, pull back off to the open string, and repeat as fast as possible. Afterward, Gtr. 1 continues on with a thick, ballsy fill from the open-position E minor pentatonic scale:

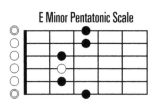

E Minor Pentatonic Scale

Meanwhile, Gtr. 2 simply chimes in to accent the E–D chord move with single-note slides.

Cocaine
Riff

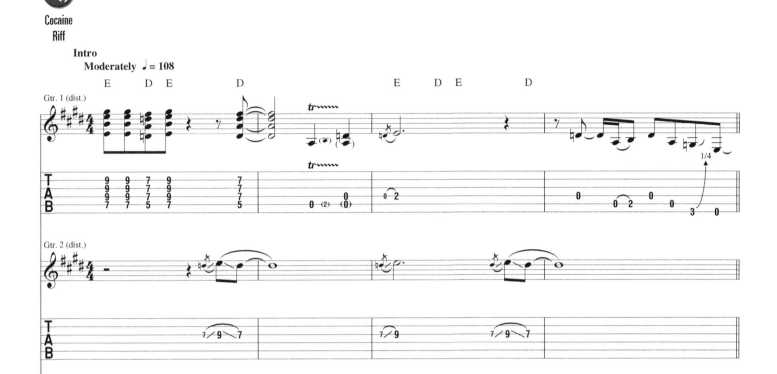

# "Lay Down Sally"
## From *Slowhand*, 1977

Another classic from the *Slowhand* album, "Lay Down Sally" represents Clapton's country rock side and features one of his most groovin', infectious riffs on record. Its easy beat is guaranteed to get heads bobbin' and feet tappin'.

The intro riff is comprised of two separate-but-equal parts: a bass line part, and a chordal/single-note hook. The tonality here is A Mixolydian, which is just like the A major scale, except the seventh tone, normally G♯, has been lowered to G.

Gtr. 2 provides the framework with a two-measure bass line riff played predominantly on strings 5 and 6. Note that the part is palm-muted throughout, which helps set it apart from Gtr. 1. After the open fifth string, begin with your index finger taking fret 2 on string 6 and your middle finger taking the final note of the measure—fret 2 on string 4. This will allow you to easily add the ring finger for fret 3 on string 6. Maintain those finger assignments throughout the entire riff. Regarding the picking, use downstrokes for all the notes except those on string 4, which will be upstrokes. The picking pattern may take a bit of getting used to, so start slowly and work on it until it's automatic before increasing the tempo.

Gtr. 1 adds the spice and the ear candy on top. After pecking out a barred A chord in open position, slightly release the pressure but remain touching the strings to create the deadened notes on beats 2.5 and 3 of the first measure, reasserting pressure once again for the double stops on the 2nd fret of strings 4 and 3 that follow.

Measure 2 contains the hippest part of this whole riff. Alternating against the open G string as a pedal tone, play G on string 4, fret 5 and then F♯ at fret 4, both with the ring finger, grabbing the A note at fret 2, string 3 at the end of the measure with the index finger. Be sure to keep your ring finger arched so that the open G string is allowed to ring (see photo).

In measure 3, he follows more 2nd-fret double stops and scratch (dead) notes with a slow bend on fret 3, string 6 with the middle finger. And he rounds out the phrase in measure 4, answering the 2nd-fret double stop and scratch notes this time with a pull-off from fret 4 to 2 on the fourth string.

One thing of note here is that, while the bass line riff (Gtr. 2) is comprised of a two-measure-structure, the "lead" riff (Gtr. 1) is composed of a four-measure structure, which is an interesting way to get more mileage out of the same material.

# "Forever Man"
## From *Behind the Sun*, 1985

Clapton had a few hit or miss years in the early '80s, but "Forever Man," from 1985's *Behind the Sun*, became a hit for him at #26, which pushed the album up to #34. This was the first sign of his eventual comeback, which would be more fully realized with 1989's Grammy-winning *Journeyman*. This involved revamping his sound with the incorporation of synthesizers and a glossier production, but his inimitable guitar playing always remained at the heart of the sound.

For the intro riff to "Forever Man," Clapton's tuned to drop D tuning. This simply involves lowering the pitch of your sixth string from E down a whole step to D. If you're without a tuner, a quick and dirty way to get there is to lower your sixth string until the sound matches your open fourth string (your sixth will be one octave lower than the fourth).

The riff, from the D minor pentatonic scale, takes place entirely on the bottom two strings and grooves hard. The D minor pentatonic can be played with a neat, symmetrical fingering with this tuning, which is quite handy for riffs such as these.

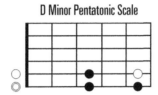

D Minor Pentatonic Scale

To fatten it up, the riff is doubled by a synth on the recording, but it sounds great on its own as well. It's quite syncopated, so if you're having trouble reading the rhythms, listen closely to the audio to get a feel for it. Aside from the open string notes, you can remain in third position for the entirety of the riff.

Gtr. 2 adds another texture to the riff by alternating muted dead notes against ♭7th (C) notes in a 16th-note rhythm. *Alternate pick* these (continuous up and down picking) with a slight palm mute to achieve the right effect. This is similar to strumming a chord in a continuous rhythm, but here you're focusing on just one string while fretting and releasing the C notes.

The most difficult aspect of the main riff is likely to be the trill on beat 4. Trills are never easy, but this one is interesting because it's followed by the open low D string. So you have to feel how to time the ending of it. You don't want to quit too early and leave one of the notes hanging out, but you don't want it to bleed over the open sixth string either. This will just take some repetition, but eventually you'll get a feel for it.

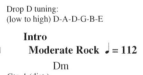

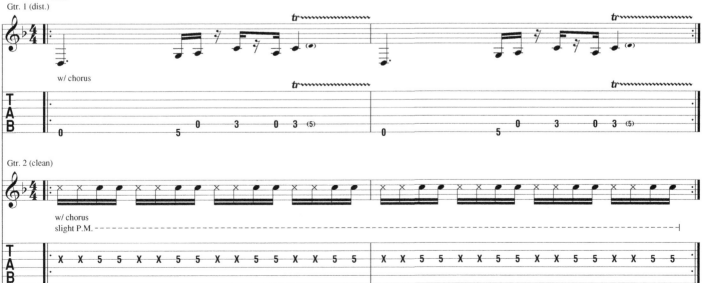

# "Bad Love"
## From *Journeyman*, 1989

By the end of the '80s, Clapton had found success again with a newly refined sound, and *Journeyman* marked the beginning of a healthy streak of success that continued long into the next decade, though the glossy production of the album wouldn't be repeated. The stripped down aesthetic of his monumentally successful *Unplugged* album in 1992 would be transferred to the ultra-raw electric triumph, *From the Cradle*, in 1994, reasserting his place among the top for fans everywhere after his wayward explorations through the '80s.

"Bad Love" begins with a synth intro, but Clapton follows it up with this classic riff. Working from the D minor pentatonic scale almost exclusively and using a wah pedal throughout, he sets the tone for things to come. He employs an extended one-octave form of the scale, making use of slides to change positions instead of remaining in one position. It looks like this:

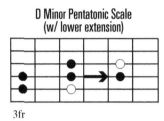

D Minor Pentatonic Scale
(w/ lower extension)

3fr

As such, you can get away with playing most of this riff using your index and ring fingers only. Begin in third position for the two pickup notes on string 5. On the downbeat of measure 1, slide with your ring finger from fret 5 to 7 on string 4 and grab fret 5 on string 3 with your index before sliding your ring finger back down to fret 5. Remain in third position through the end of measure 2. After sliding up to fifth position and back down again in measure 3, Clapton works his way down a few double stops on strings 4 and 3 before landing on the 5th fret of strings 5 and 4, where he slides up a whole step and quickly returns.

Measures 5–6 are essentially a repeat of 1–2, but in measure 7, Clapton ascends to the high D on string 3 with the ring finger before sliding back down to third position. He finishes it off with a syncopated B♭ chord, with the ring finger on fret 5, string 5 and the index finger barring fret 3 on strings 4 and 3.

This song is an interesting synthesis of his old and new (at the time) style. While the production is certainly of the late '80s, the writing and arranging harkens back to his earlier days. Think about it: the song starts with a D minor pentatonic riff and then moves to the distant key of B minor for the verse (not shown). "Layla" also starts off with D minor pentatonic riffs and then moves to a distant key (C♯ minor) for the verse. And in the middle, the song breaks down and picks up with a descending arpeggio riff in D which sets up the solo. One can't help but notice the similarity to "Badge" in this regard. Food for thought!

# *"Old Love"*
## From *Journeyman*, 1989

You'd think that Clapton would just about have given up on love after *Journeyman*, what with the "Bad Love" and "Old Love" through which he was wading. The latter song he co-wrote with the inimitable Robert Cray and is yet another product of Clapton's relationship with Pattie Boyd—this time a regretful tale of a break-up.

The song, which is in A minor, begins with two clean guitars panned hard left and right playing similar parts. Gtr. 1 is treated to a subtle amp tremolo, which results in an ever-so-slight pulsating effect. The riff is a masterful combination of single-note bass-register lines and chords.

Begin by sliding your ring finger from fret 5 to 7 on the fifth string, taking notice of the staccato mark on the E note, which really helps the riff groove. This will put you in fifth position—perfect for the following Am and Dm7 chords:

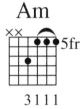

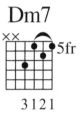

The next two chords, G7sus4 and G, take place in third position:

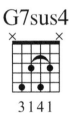

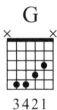

For the second single-note line, slide into fret 7 on string 5 the same way as before, but then shift down to fret 5 with the ring finger. This will put you in third position for the rest of the line. Again, take note of the same staccato mark on the first E note. All the single-note lines taken together come from the A minor pentatonic scale and can be thought of as this extended A minor pentatonic scale form, which can be fingered entirely with the index and ring finger via a slide on string 5:

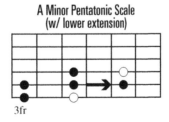

Gtr. 2 plays a slight variation in measures 2 and 3. In measure 2, the single-note line is played the same, but up one octave. The fingering lays out exactly the same as Gtr. 1, but here in seventh and fifth positions. Then, in measure 3, instead of mimicking the more simplistic Gtr. 1 chord strums, Gtr. 2 arpeggiates up the Am chord, stepping very smoothly into the subsequent Dm7 chord strum.

The slow tempo means that none of this is very challenging in a technical sense, but it makes timing issues even more apparent. So what's lacking in technical challenges is made up for in timing. This riff needs to sit in the pocket to really groove!

**Old Love**
**Riff**

**Intro**
**Moderately slow** ♩ = 70

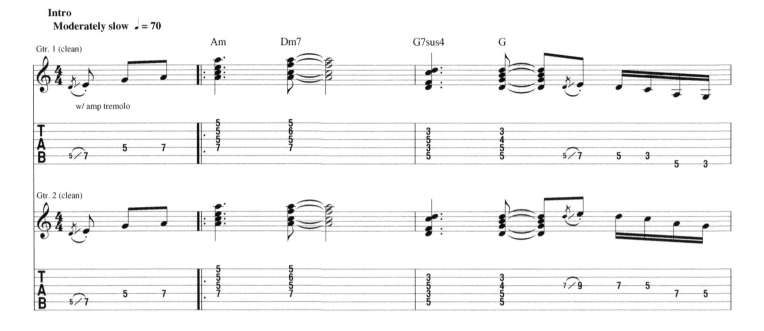

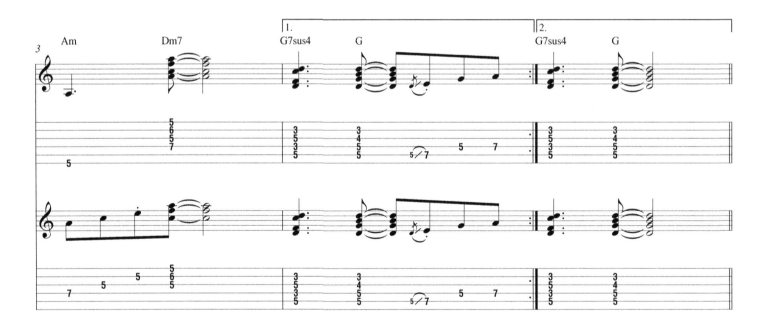

# "Change the World"
## featured on the Motion Picture Soundtrack *Phenomenon*, 1996

Clapton teamed up with Babyface to record this acoustic track for the 1996 film *Phenomenon*, yet another in his long line of soundtrack contributions. The move turned out to be a smart one, as the song reached #5 on the charts and helped push the album to #12. Though firmly rooted in the adult contemporary genre, the song nevertheless features some extremely tasty acoustic playing by Eric.

Clapton kicks off the song with a great fingerstyle chordal riff in E that works its way up from E to F#m7 and Gadd9 before coming back down in similar fashion. (Note that after the Intro, Clapton changes the riff to a more simplified dyad progression on strings 3 and 5.) As Clapton is fingerpicking, he targets specific strings in these chord voicings, illustrated here:

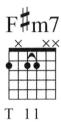
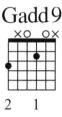

Although Clapton is specific with regards to his plucking in measures 1, 3, and 5, when he's transitioning up or down through the three chords, he's not so much in measures 2, 4, or 6, when he's hanging out on one chord (either E or Gadd9) for the full measure. What you should take from this is that, while it makes sense to learn the former note for note, don't worry too much about being exact for the latter. Also note that this is an arrangement of two guitars playing a very similar part, panned right and left on the original recording.

With regards to the plucking hand, the constant is that you'll use your thumb throughout on string 6. For the notes on the other strings, there's room for experimentation to see what feels best, so try several things out. In measure 4, Clapton decorates the open E chord with a quick hammer-pull move on string 1 with the open string and the 2nd fret. The pinky finger seems like the logical choice on the fret hand for this.

After basically repeating measures 1–3 for measures 5–7, Clapton hits a syncopated B7sus4 chord at the end of measure 7 to signal the end of the section. The only logical fingering for this chord seems to be index, pinky, middle (low to high).

Change the World
Riff

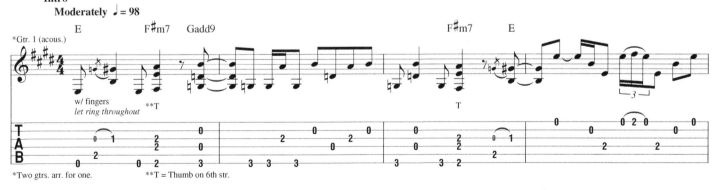

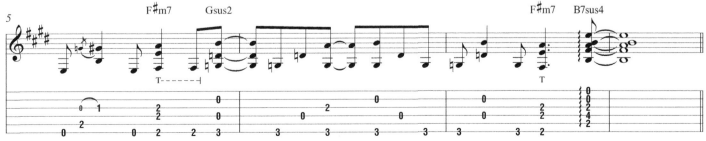

# INTEGRAL TECHNIQUES

It's interesting that the word "technical" often takes on a negative connotation with regards to more emotionally-charged music like the blues. You may hear disparaging remarks like, "He's too technical; he has no soul." The funny thing is that, in the strict sense of the word, blues guitar is *predominantly* about technique. Just because it's not classical technique, for example, doesn't make it any less valid. Blues and rock guitar have their own set of technical demands and necessities, and those techniques have an equal, if not *greater*, impact on the sound than the actual notes do.

To put it another way, blues/blues rock guitar would not sound the way it does without the guitar techniques used to create it: string bending, vibrato, varied pick attack, fret-hand muting, etc. All of these are issues of technique. And so when someone says something like Eric Clapton or Stevie Ray Vaughan aren't "technical" players (or weren't in Stevie's case), they're missing a huge piece of the puzzle. Eric plays, and Stevie certainly played, with an enormous amount of technique; it just happens to be refined and geared toward the type of music they play. That said, let's examine some of the integral parts of Clapton's technique and see how they help shape and define his sound.

## Vibrato

One of the biggest pieces of the Clapton sonic puzzle has to be his glorious vibrato. Ever since his days with the Bluesbreakers, and especially his time with Cream, Clapton's vibrato has stood out as one of the most musical around. While most rock or blues players, including Hendrix, B.B. King, Stevie Ray Vaughan, among many others, use a wrist motion to create vibrato, Clapton is different in this regard. He actually generates his main vibrato motion by moving his forearm and leaving his wrist locked.

For example, let's look at a classic note to which he'll add vibrato, which would be the minor 3rd on string 3 in a standard minor pentatonic box. In the key of D, for instance, that would be this note here:

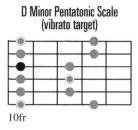

D Minor Pentatonic Scale
(vibrato target)

10fr

This note would be played with the index finger. To generate the vibrato, Clapton would take his thumb off the neck completely so that only the tip of his index finger is making contact with the string (see photos). He would then move the forearm to generate a slight upward bend of about a quarter step, release it, and repeat over and over quickly.

Here's what this would sound like in a typical lick.

Techniques
Example 1

This is the type of vibrato he'll apply to any unbent note with the index, middle, or ring finger on the top three strings. And if you spend any time watching him play, you'll notice that he usually adds vibrato with his index or middle (when not bending).

However, when applying vibrato to the lower strings—especially the fifth and sixth—he'll use more of a standard wrist-type rock vibrato. In this instance, he'll keep his thumb touching the top of the neck (see photos) and will slightly rotate the wrist to create the vibrato. This type is generally more subtle than that which he uses on the upper strings, but it's no less effective.

And here's how this type of vibrato would sound in a typical lick.

Techniques
Example 2

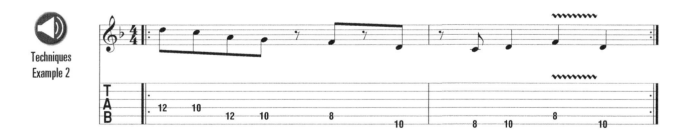

Eric would also, of course, add vibrato to bent notes as well, but we'll take a look at that in the next section.

# *String Bending*

Any blues player worth his salt needs to learn the art of string bending, and Clapton is no slouch at all in this department. And even more so than his vibrato, his bending technique is quite unorthodox. Let's take a closer look.

Clapton bends strings mostly with his ring and middle fingers on the higher strings. When bending with his ring ringer, he actually does not use a supporting finger behind it (see photo). This is quite unusual and very difficult if you've never done it.

If you didn't happen to learn this way, there's no reason to try it, because tonally speaking, there shouldn't be any difference. But it's quite an interesting fact.

Clapton is almost exclusively a three-finger player when it comes to lead playing (though he does make use of his pinky often for chords). When playing licks out of the typical minor pentatonic box shape, he'll usually bend strings 2 and 1 with the ring finger and string 3 with the middle. For instance, in the key of C, the box would be in eighth position. Clapton would normally bend fret 11 on string 2 and string 1 with the ring finger. For fret 10 on string 3, he'd most likely use the middle finger. He also almost always anchors his thumb over the top of the neck when bending.

Techniques
Example 3

The exception to this is when he's playing in a very low position on the neck. If he's in third position playing out of the G minor pentatonic box, for instance, he may use his ring finger for the bend on fret 5, string 3. Also, when playing out of other scale forms, such as the "B.B. box," he may bend on string 2 with the middle finger.

## Overbend

Another thing Clapton makes use of on occasion is the *overbend*. This is a bend that's stretched more than a whole step. The most common are one and a half steps and two steps. Depending on your string gauge, this can take some considerable finger strength, so supporting your bending finger with another behind it (even though Clapton doesn't) is definitely recommended! Here's an example of a typical lick using a two-step bend.

Techniques
Example 4

## Unison Bend

The *unison bend* is another Clapton favorite—especially in his earlier work. To perform a unison bend, we play a note on a lower string and another on a higher string simultaneously; then we bend the note on the lower string up to match the pitch of the one on the higher string. Probably the most famous unison bend of all involves bending the ♭7th of a minor pentatonic scale up to match the root note in the standard box shape. In the key of E minor, for instance, that would involve these two notes of the shape in 12th position:

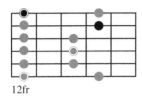

It'll take some practice at first to get the feel for it. As the bend approaches the pitch of the higher string, you'll begin to hear the "beats" (pulses) slow down—just as when you're tuning your open strings. When they stop, you've got the bend right in tune. Try it out with this lick:

Techniques
Example 5

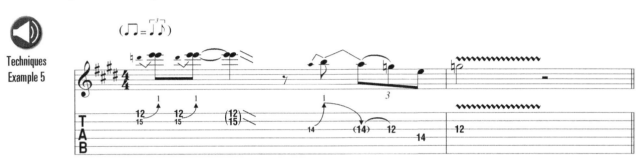

## Pre-Bend

The *pre-bend* is another technique that Clapton has mastered. The idea here is to silently bend a string before picking it. You can then simply hold it, add vibrato to it, release it, or even bend it up farther. Clapton usually does one of the first three options.

Let's start with a whole-step pre-bend on string 2 as an example. We'll bend fret 11, a B♭, up to C. First, play a C note at fret 8 on string 1 to hear the pitch. Then, try pre-bending string 2 at fret 11 to match that pitch.

Techniques
Example 6

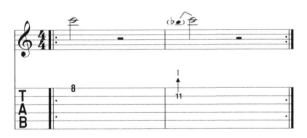

Notice that, in the tab, the pre-bend is indicated with a vertical arrow instead of a curved one. Now play the same pre-bend and release it, like this:

Techniques
Example 7

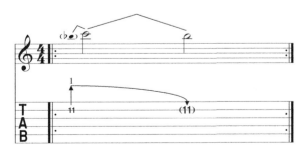

Eric will often perform several pre-bends in a row of different amounts to generate licks like these. You'll need to really have the technique down in order to achieve his precision.

Techniques
Example 8

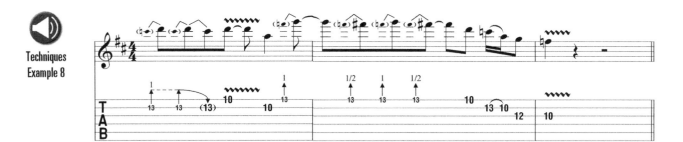

## Adding Vibrato to Bent Notes

Clapton is also a master at adding vibrato to a bent note. This is most often done on a whole-step bend performed with the middle or ring finger, but there are exceptions to this, of course. To create vibrato on a bent note, Clapton would first bend the note to pitch (see photos), release it almost back to the starting point, and bend it back to pitch over and over.

He wouldn't do this extremely quickly; it's a bit slower than most people, which is one of the reasons that it's so smooth sounding. Here's how it sounds in a typical lick using the E minor pentatonic box in 12th position.

Techniques
Example 9

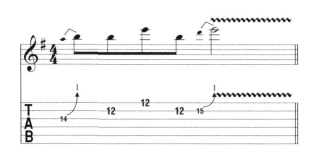

Listen to the early Cream albums to hear some really great examples of this technique.

# Tremolo Picking

Another trick Clapton has up his sleeve is *tremolo picking*. He'll often use this in a slow blues when he really starts cooking. Tremolo picking is a simple concept: you simply pick a note (or notes) as fast as you can over and over. The technique, however, is not quite as easy. Every player tremolo picks in a different manner, and many players adopt a totally different picking motion than usual when they tremolo pick. Eddie Van Halen is a prime example, as he completely arches his wrist out from the face of the guitar and flicks it back and forth rapidly to achieve the sound.

Clapton is another example of this. While his motion is not as greatly altered, he'll usually move his palm back behind the bridge and slightly arch his wrist a bit more than normal while tremolo picking. This means that he'll be picking the strings closer to the bridge, which accomplishes two things:

- It produces a brighter, edgier tone.
- The string tension will feel tighter, which makes it easier for the pick to glide through the strings.

The second point may sound counterintuitive, but think about it this way. When there's a lot of give to the string—as there is when picking near the neck—the pick has to travel farther before the string will slip off it and snap back to its original position. When picking near the bridge, the string won't give much before it slips off the pick.

Clapton actually tends to use this technique most often with double stops. Here's a typical way in which he'll use tremolo picking, which makes use of the extended box position of the D minor pentatonic scale and the D Dorian mode (for the G/B double stop).

Techniques
Example 10

You'll most likely need to experiment to find a picking motion that works well for you when tremolo picking. Every player is different, and there's no one right method. But it's a great sound to have in your bag of tricks, so it's definitely worth the effort.

# Trills, Mordents & Turns

These are all ornaments that help dress up a phrase here and there. They can be subtle or more pronounced, but in any case, you'd miss them if they weren't there.

## Trill

A *trill* is the rapid alteration between any two notes. On the guitar, this is often done in the key of E in open position involving an open string and a fretted note with alternated hammer-ons and pull-offs. Here's a common example of that. Most people, including Eric, would use the middle finger for the hammering and pull-off.

Techniques
Example 11

The other type of trill is one in which both notes are fretted. This is almost always done with the index for the lower note, and the middle or ring usually frets the higher note. Here's a typical example of that; we're using a half-step trill in this case, which would be accomplished with the index and middle fingers.

**Techniques
Example 12**

Trills are not easy—especially to make sound effortless the way Clapton, Hendrix, and Stevie Ray have—so you'll need to be patient and practice them if you want to achieve good results!

## Mordents & Turns

A *mordent* is similar to a trill, but instead of alternating between two notes over and over, you only do it once. In other words, you pick a note, hammer on to a higher note, and then pull back off to the lower note. Or you could pick a note, pull off to a lower note, and then hammer back on to the higher note. Clapton uses the former method much more frequently.

Here's how a mordent would sound in a typical lick from C minor pentatonic, using what's known as box 3 of the scale. The scale form looks like this:

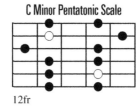

C Minor Pentatonic Scale

12fr

**Techniques
Example 13**

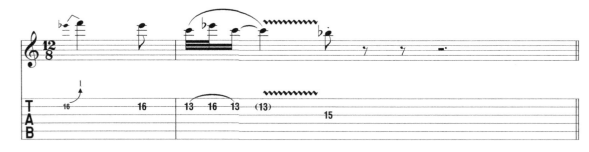

A *turn* takes the mordent idea one step further. This is the ornament you'll hear Clapton do most of all. With a turn, you basically perform an upper mordent (alternating with a note above) and then a lower mordent all in one move. So instead of just, for example, C–E♭–C, as in our previous mordent example, a turn would continue the move so that we'd get C–E♭–C–B♭–C (using the C minor pentatonic scale as our melodic base).

The rhythm of the notes can be varied a bit, but in Clapton's case, they're usually spaced fairly evenly, although sometimes the first three notes (the upper mordent portion) may be slightly faster than the lower portion. Here's another lick from the same C minor pentatonic position that demonstrates a typical Clapton turn.

Techniques
Example 14

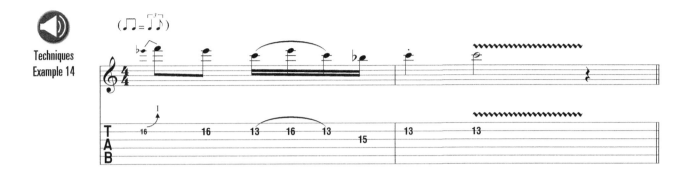

## *Repetitive Licks*

Clapton will often turn a turn (no pun intended) into a repetitive lick by repeating it over and over. The previous lick is a perfect example. If we play that over and over, we'll get something that Clapton might do.

Techniques
Example 15

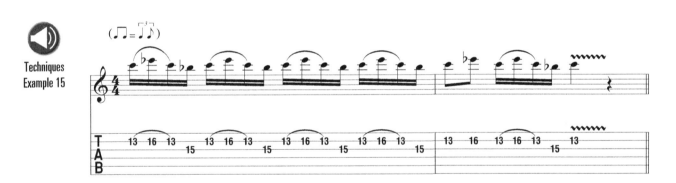

He'll often stretch this idea out over several measures when he's really cooking, and he can really fly through these types of things. It's also worth mentioning that, as we talked about in the tremolo picking section, Clapton will tend to pick closer to the bridge the faster he plays. This is most likely instinctual, but it makes sense from a technical standpoint.

Another repetitive lick that Clapton likes to use is not a mordent or a turn, but it's simply a three-note pull-off lick from the minor pentatonic box. In D, this would take place in 10th position, and a typical lick might go like this:

Techniques
Example 16

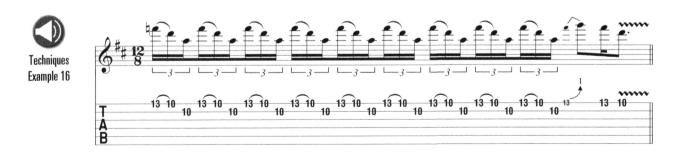

# STYLISTIC DNA

In this section we'll dig a bit deeper and look for some common threads running through Clapton's guitar work that help us recognize him. A lot of these ideas may be subtle, but in reality, subtlety is what distinguishes most blues players from each other. When you consider how many blues players have used similar gear and similar melodic material (i.e., the blues scale), this becomes a bit more evident.

## Lower Extension Boxes of the Minor Pentatonic Scale

Clapton is almost exclusively a three-finger player when it comes to lead (though he does often make use of his pinky for chords). As such, he's developed ways to avoid the use of his pinky and/or the awkward stretches that would occur if he substituted the ring finger. A perfect case in point is use of the lower extension box in the minor pentatonic scale.

To start, let's take a look at the typical A minor pentatonic box in fifth position. Clapton will readily play every one of these notes except one, which is indicated by a grey dot.

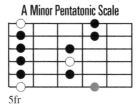

In order to play that low C note on string 6, he'd need to either use his pinky or stretch out with his ring finger. Neither choice is consistent with the angled grip that he uses when normally fretting notes.

Instead, to avoid this, Clapton makes use of the lower extension box, which looks like this in the key of A:

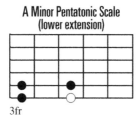

In order to connect the two, he'll use a slide on string 5, such as this:

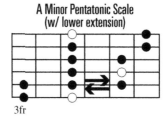

Here's how this might sound in a typical lick. In this instance, you'd begin in third position with your ring finger on fret 5.

This also applies to the minor pentatonic form with its tonic on the fifth string, which is sometimes referred to as box 4 (with the standard "box" shape being box 1). In A, this would be open or 12th position. We'll demonstrate in 12th position here. Again, you're unlikely to ever see Clapton play the notes at the positions indicated with grey dots.

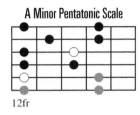

Instead, he makes use of this lower extension box, which would put us in 10th position:

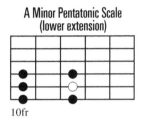

Putting it all together, we can see how he slides up or down to join the two:

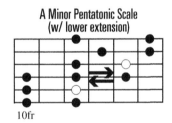

Here's a typical lick in A that demonstrates this concept.

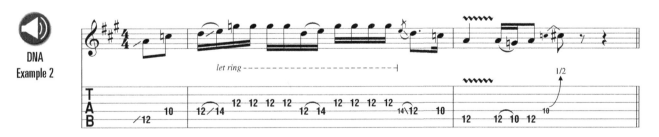

Again, this is a subtle thing, but that slide—ascending or descending—has become a characteristic sound in Clapton's style and really helps in achieving the fluidity for which he's known.

## Starting with a Unison Bend

This is something that Clapton made frequent use of especially in the early days—with the Bluesbreakers, for instance. He'd often make his entrance into a solo loud and proud with a unison bend. Most often, this bend would be one of two kinds: a whole-step bend from the ♭7th of the scale up to the tonic, or a whole-step bend from the 4th to the 5th. They would also almost always take place on either the 3/2 string group or 2/1 string group.

Here's an example from the E minor pentatonic scale in which we're bending up from the ♭7th (D) to the root (E) on string 1 while fretting E on string 1. This lick comes from the standard E minor pentatonic box shape in 12th position. Regarding the vibrato on the unison bend, don't worry about the stationary note; only add vibrato to the bent note, and the desired effect will be achieved. Here's the scale:

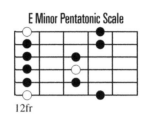

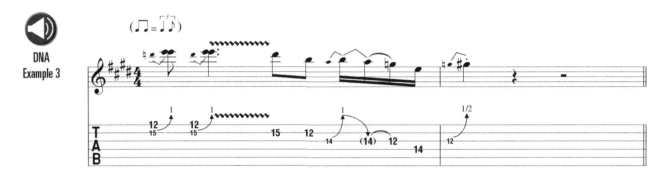

And here's another similar idea from the same scale form. This time, we're bending string 3 from the 4th (A) up to the 5th (B) while fretting B on string 2.

This is an idea that you would especially hear Clapton do at the beginning of a second solo if he had two in one song. And the unison bend doesn't always have to be struck simultaneously, either. Another variation that Clapton used often is the more melodic version of it. In this lick, hold the bend and allow it to ring while you're picking the 12th fret on string 2.

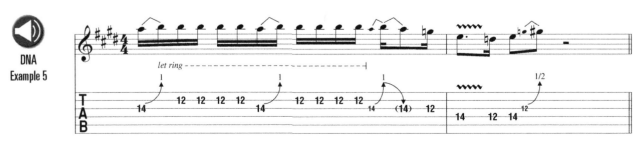

# Use of the Major 7th

Another of Clapton's go-to sounds is his use of the major 7th instead of the minor 7th, as is found in the minor pentatonic scale. This is a sound that was commonly heard in the playing of the Delta slide players of the '30s and '40s, but all but vanished from modern electric blues. Clapton was one of the proponents of this very hip sound.

He almost always uses it the same way: as a lower neighbor tone to the tonic. And he almost always uses it in the same scale form, which is box 4 of the minor pentatonic scale. For example, in the key of G, the normal minor pentatonic scale, box 4, would look like this:

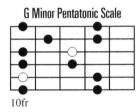

However, on string 3, Clapton will often just briefly play the F♯ on fret 11, string 3 instead of F at fret 10:

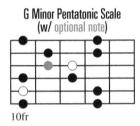

Here's a typical example of how this may sound.

**DNA Example 6**

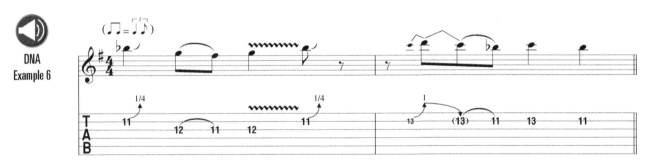

Or this can be more of a slow blues thing, such as this example from the same position.

**DNA Example 7**

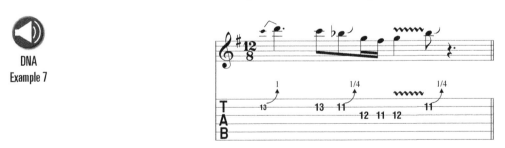

Aside from the fact that Eric obviously heard this sound in plenty of old Delta blues recordings, it's also a convenient result of his fingering. Since Clapton would always use his index on fret 11, string 2 in this scale form, he'll often use his middle finger on string 3, fret 12. This means that reaching back for F at fret 10 would be an awkward stretch, so the F♯ is actually easier. (The exception to this is when he's descending from this note, in which case he'd shift to his ring finger for fret 12, string 3.)

# ♭3 – 1 – 4 – 1

This small lick fragment, and slight variations of it, shows up all over Eric's improvisations, particularly in slow blues songs. These numbers refer to scale degrees of the minor pentatonic scale. If you were to give each of the five notes a number, or degree, you'd say the scale would be "spelled" 1–♭3–4–5–♭7.

He most often plays this fragment in the standard minor pentatonic box. So, in the key of A, for instance, that would be the shape shown here in fifth position. These four notes—the 1, ♭3, and 4—will be shown as grey in the diagram. They would be the notes A (1), C (♭3), and D (4). So, basically, the idea is to quickly pivot off the 1 with the ♭3 and 4 notes.

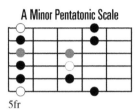

So here's how you may see this little idea in a typical lick from this A minor pentatonic box in fifth position. In beat 2 of this lick, where the fragment lies, Clapton would most likely use his index finger for fret 5, string 3, his middle finger for fret 7, string 4, and his ring finger for fret 7, string 3.

DNA

Example 8

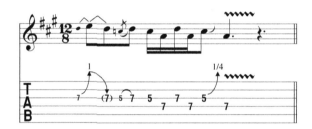

And here's an example of how he may use this idea in a more uptempo shuffle. We'll be playing out of the E minor pentatonic box in 12th position this time.

DNA

Example 9

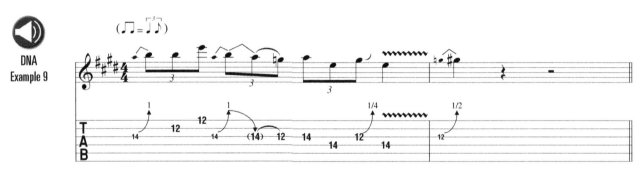

You'll hear variations of this idea all over the place in Eric's playing if you listen closely. It's a great little juggling of notes that helps prevent things from sounding too predictable.

# *Mixing Major and Minor Pentatonic Sounds*

This is one of the most prominent ideas that helped set Clapton apart in the early days. While other guitarists of the day, such as Hendrix, certainly made use of both major and minor pentatonic sounds, few would blend them as seamlessly and fluidly as Eric. He would often switch between the two at the drop of a hat in the middle of a phrase, which gave his playing freshness and a continued element of surprise.

Let's take a look at this idea in the key of A. In a typical blues rock song in A, you may find many phrases based out of this A minor pentatonic box in 17th position:

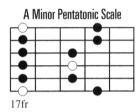

Clapton, however, would also mix notes in from the parallel A major pentatonic scale, which would look like this in that same basic position:

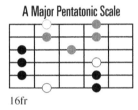

The grey notes in the diagram represent the ones that Clapton would frequently use. The major pentatonic notes in the lower octave would hardly, if ever, be used. Let's take a look at a typical lick that demonstrates how he might switch between the two scales in one phrase.

He would also mix notes from both scales freely throughout one phrase. Here's an example of that in the same position.

This is still, to this day, an underused strategy in blues and blues rock playing, even though Clapton set such a beautiful example nearly 50 years ago.

## Repeated Groups of Four in a Triplet Phrase

This is a nifty little trick that you'll hear Clapton use most often in a moderate-to-uptempo shuffle feel. The idea is to play straight triplets, or three notes per beat, but repeat a four-note group. This means that the accent (i.e., the beginning of the four-note group) will shift to a different triplet each time the lick is repeated.

Here's a classic example from the C minor pentatonic box in eighth position. The four-note group is marked each time.

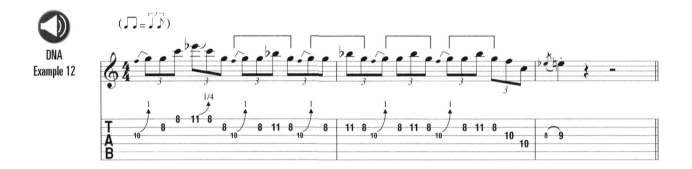

This is easier said than done, because it's very easy to either lose your place in the measure or get off beat when playing this idea. So it'll take a bit of practice to be able to feel it correctly.

## Index-Finger Bend Followed by Middle/Ring Finger

This is a common theme running through many of Clapton's solos, yet it doesn't draw that much attention to itself, even though it's not all that subtle. The idea is to bend string 3 with your index finger in the minor pentatonic box and follow it with the middle or ring finger two frets higher. In key of D, for instance, we'd be talking about the scale form in 10th position, as shown in this diagram (the specific notes shown in grey):

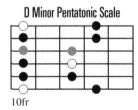

D Minor Pentatonic Scale

10fr

In this case, we're talking about fretting the F on string 3 with our index finger and the G with our middle or ring finger. The idea is to give the index-finger note a slight bend—usually either a quarter step or a half step—and follow it with an unbent note two frets higher. Clapton often repeats this move over and over. Here's a typical idea using the D scale form.

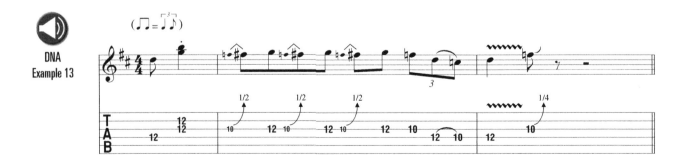

This idea can have a quirkier sound in the hands of someone like Jeff Beck, but Clapton manages to make it a bit more understated.

# Verses in Non-Related Keys

This is more of a songwriting trait, but it occurs in many of Clapton's original songs and is therefore worth noting. Often times Clapton will begin a song with an intro riff that will come back as the chorus or some other important part, but in between, there will be a verse that changes to a completely different key in a somewhat jarring fashion.

For instance, he may kick off a song with a riff in D minor, but then move to the key of A major for the verses. Here's an example of how this may sound.

**DNA Example 14**

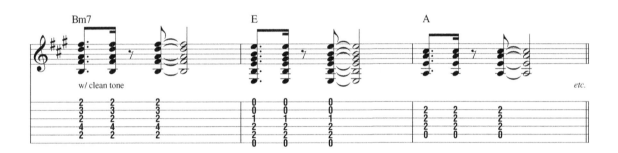

# *MUST HEAR*

With a career as long as Eric's, you end up leaving quite an audio trail. Clapton's is filled with some of the most classic rock and blues music around. Let's check out some of the absolute essential listening with regard to Slowhand.

## *Bluesbreakers with Eric Clapton, 1966*

### Essential tracks

Hide Away
Double Crossing Time
Little Girl
Steppin' Out

## *Fresh Cream, 1966*

### Essential Tracks

I Feel Free
N.S.U.
Spoonful

## *Disraeli Gears, 1967*

### Essential Tracks

Strange Brew
Sunshine of Your Love
Tales of Brave Ulysses
SWLABR

## *Wheels of Fire, 1968*

### Essential Tracks

White Room
Crossroads
Sitting on Top of the World
As You Said
Politician

## *Goodbye, 1969*

### Essential Tracks

Badge
I'm So Glad

## *Blind Faith, 1969*

**Essential Tracks**

In the Presence of the Lord
Can't Find My Way Home
Do What You Like

## *Layla and Other Assorted Love Songs, 1970*

**Essential Tracks**

Everything!

## *Eric Clapton, 1970*

**Essential Tracks**

Let It Rain
After Midnight
Slunky
Bad Boy

## *461 Ocean Boulevard, 1974*

**Essential Tracks**

Motherless Children
I Shot the Sheriff
Let It Grow

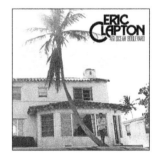

## *There's One in Every Crowd, 1975*

**Essential Tracks**

The Sky Is Crying

## *E.C. Was Here, 1975*

**Essential Tracks**

Rambling on My Mind
Further on up the Road

## *No Reason to Cry, 1976*

**Essential Tracks**

Sign Language
Double Trouble

## *Slowhand, 1977*

**Essential Tracks**

Cocaine
Lay Down Sally
Wonderful Tonight

## *Behind the Sun, 1985*

**Essential Tracks**

Forever Man

## *August, 1986*

**Essential Tracks**

It's in the Way That You Use It

## *Journeyman, 1989*

**Essential Tracks**

Pretending
Bad Love
Running on Faith
Hard Times
Old Love
Before You Accuse Me

## *24 Nights, 1991*

**Essential Tracks**

White Room
Sunshine of Your Love

## Rush (Soundtrack), 1992

### Essential Tracks

Tracks and Lines
Tears in Heaven

## Unplugged, 1992

### Essential Tracks

Layla
Walkin' Blues
Before You Accuse Me
Old Love

## From the Cradle, 1994

### Essential Tracks

I'm Tore Down
It Hurts Me Too
Third Degree
Groaning the Blues

## Me and Mr. Johnson, 2004

### Essential Tracks

Kind Hearted Woman Blues
Come on in My Kitchen

## Clapton, 2010

### Essential Tracks

Travelin' Alone
Rocking Chair

# MUST SEE

Seeing a player in action can often answer many specific questions about techniques, preferences, and more, so it would behoove any serious Clapton fan to dig in to these excellent video performances.

## On DVD

### Cream: Farewell Concert, 2005

Warning: This is a DVD of Cream's farewell concert, which was filmed at the Royal Albert Hall on November 26, 1968. Though it sounds like a dream come true, it's extremely frustrating for a guitar player (or a drummer or bassist, for that matter) to watch. Most of the video, believe it or not, features close-ups of their faces. On the rare occurrence that you do get a look at the hands, it's often the back of the neck. The audio is perfectly listenable, though, and there is some fierce playing indeed. There is, however, an extremely nice, brief interview with Eric where he demonstrates various techniques, concepts, etc. on his "Fool" SG. But this interview is also available on YouTube (see below).

### *Eric Clapton & Friends: Live 1986*

### *24 Nights*, 1990

### *The Cream of Eric Clapton*, 1990

### *Unplugged*, 1992

*Sessions for Robert J.*, 2004 (CD/DVD combo)

*Cream – Royal Albert Hall – London May 2-3-5-6 2005*

*Crossroads Guitar Festival 2010*

# *On YouTube*

Use the following search terms to find these essential Clapton nuggets.

### Cream Farewell Concert 1968 – Eric Clapton Interview

This is the Clapton interview from 1968 that appeared on the DVD, *Cream: Farewell Concert*. It lasts almost five minutes, and you get to hear Clapton explain his tone controls, vibrato, picking nuance, and more, in his own words, with beautifully performed examples of each.

### Cream – Live in Alameda County, Oakland 1968

This is an audio-only bootleg concert with more than decent sound quality and some exceptional playing by all three members.

### Derek and the Dominos Live on Johnny Cash

This is just delightful. Clapton and the gang play some country rock songs on the Johnny Cash show, circa November 1970. It's a testament to Clapton's versatility as a player, as he pulls off some fairly legitimate-sounding country licks here with a sweet Strat tone.

### Blind Faith – Can't Find My Way Home – 1969

This is Blind Faith live at Hyde Park in London in June of 1969. It's not the best video of Clapton, as he's often behind the drums, but there's some great playing, and you get several good looks at Clapton's Telecaster.

## Little Wing (1970) by Derek and the Dominos Live

This is an audio-only (with slide show) version of the Dominos covering the Hendrix classic in 1970. There's some fabulous singing by Clapton and Whitlock and of course some incredible guitar playing as well.

## Eric Clapton: Nothing but the Blues

*Nothing but the Blues* is a documentary directed by Martin Scorsese. It was broadcast on PBS but never released commercially, which is a real shame, because it features lots of interviews with Clapton and other blues greats. But mainly it includes many live performances from an early-to-mid '90s Clapton concert, and the man is simply *on fire* in just about every single one of them. From the main search, you should be able to get to most of the show, but specifically check out "Groaning the Blues," "Ain't Nobody's Business," and "Five Long Years." Ow!

## Eric Clapton Drifting Blues 2008 Unplugged

This is Eric all by his lonesome turning out a spot-on performance of "Drifting Blues" on acoustic. You don't get this smooth and polished without years and years under your belt!

# HAL•LEONARD GUITAR PLAY-ALONG

This series will help you play your favorite songs quickly and easily. Just follow the tab and listen to the CD to the hear how the guitar should sound, and then play along using the separate backing tracks. Mac or PC users can also slow down the tempo without changing pitch by using the CD in their computer. The melody and lyrics are included in the book so that you can sing or simply follow along.

**INCLUDES TAB**

| | | |
|---|---|---|
| VOL. 1 – ROCK | 00699570 / $16.99 | |
| VOL. 2 – ACOUSTIC | 00699569 / $16.95 | |
| VOL. 3 – HARD ROCK | 00699573 / $16.95 | |
| VOL. 4 – POP/ROCK | 00699571 / $16.99 | |
| VOL. 5 – MODERN ROCK | 00699574 / $16.99 | |
| VOL. 6 – '90S ROCK | 00699572 / $16.99 | |
| VOL. 7 – BLUES | 00699575 / $16.95 | |
| VOL. 8 – ROCK | 00699585 / $14.99 | |
| VOL. 9 – PUNK ROCK | 00699576 / $14.95 | |
| VOL. 10 – ACOUSTIC | 00699586 / $16.95 | |
| VOL. 11 – EARLY ROCK | 00699579 / $14.95 | |
| VOL. 12 – POP/ROCK | 00699587 / $14.95 | |
| VOL. 13 – FOLK ROCK | 00699581 / $15.99 | |
| VOL. 14 – BLUES ROCK | 00699582 / $16.95 | |
| VOL. 15 – R&B | 00699583 / $14.95 | |
| VOL. 16 – JAZZ | 00699584 / $15.95 | |
| VOL. 17 – COUNTRY | 00699588 / $15.95 | |
| VOL. 18 – ACOUSTIC ROCK | 00699577 / $15.95 | |
| VOL. 19 – SOUL | 00699578 / $14.99 | |
| VOL. 20 – ROCKABILLY | 00699580 / $14.95 | |
| VOL. 21 – YULETIDE | 00699602 / $14.95 | |
| VOL. 22 – CHRISTMAS | 00699600 / $15.95 | |
| VOL. 23 – SURF | 00699635 / $14.95 | |
| VOL. 24 – ERIC CLAPTON | 00699649 / $17.99 | |
| VOL. 25 – LENNON & MCCARTNEY | 00699642 / $16.99 | |
| VOL. 26 – ELVIS PRESLEY | 00699643 / $14.95 | |
| VOL. 27 – DAVID LEE ROTH | 00699645 / $16.95 | |
| VOL. 28 – GREG KOCH | 00699646 / $14.95 | |
| VOL. 29 – BOB SEGER | 00699647 / $15.99 | |
| VOL. 30 – KISS | 00699644 / $16.99 | |
| VOL. 31 – CHRISTMAS HITS | 00699652 / $14.95 | |
| VOL. 32 – THE OFFSPRING | 00699653 / $14.95 | |
| VOL. 33 – ACOUSTIC CLASSICS | 00699656 / $16.95 | |
| VOL. 34 – CLASSIC ROCK | 00699658 / $16.95 | |
| VOL. 35 – HAIR METAL | 00699660 / $16.95 | |
| VOL. 36 – SOUTHERN ROCK | 00699661 / $16.95 | |
| VOL. 37 – ACOUSTIC METAL | 00699662 / $16.95 | |
| VOL. 38 – BLUES | 00699663 / $16.95 | |
| VOL. 39 – '80S METAL | 00699664 / $16.99 | |
| VOL. 40 – INCUBUS | 00699668 / $17.95 | |
| VOL. 41 – ERIC CLAPTON | 00699669 / $16.95 | |
| VOL. 42 – 2000S ROCK | 00699670 / $16.99 | |
| VOL. 43 – LYNYRD SKYNYRD | 00699681 / $17.95 | |
| VOL. 44 – JAZZ | 00699689 / $14.99 | |
| VOL. 45 – TV THEMES | 00699718 / $14.95 | |
| VOL. 46 – MAINSTREAM ROCK | 00699722 / $16.95 | |
| VOL. 47 – HENDRIX SMASH HITS | 00699723 / $19.95 | |
| VOL. 48 – AEROSMITH CLASSICS | 00699724 / $17.99 | |
| VOL. 49 – STEVIE RAY VAUGHAN | 00699725 / $17.99 | |
| VOL. 51 – ALTERNATIVE '90S | 00699727 / $14.99 | |
| VOL. 52 – FUNK | 00699728 / $14.95 | |
| VOL. 53 – DISCO | 00699729 / $14.99 | |
| VOL. 54 – HEAVY METAL | 00699730 / $14.95 | |
| VOL. 55 – POP METAL | 00699731 / $14.95 | |

| | | |
|---|---|---|
| VOL. 56 – FOO FIGHTERS | 00699749 / $15.99 | |
| VOL. 57 – SYSTEM OF A DOWN | 00699751 / $14.95 | |
| VOL. 58 – BLINK-182 | 00699772 / $14.95 | |
| VOL. 59 – CHET ATKINS | 00702347 / $16.99 | |
| VOL. 60 – 3 DOORS DOWN | 00699774 / $14.95 | |
| VOL. 61 – SLIPKNOT | 00699775 / $16.99 | |
| VOL. 62 – CHRISTMAS CAROLS | 00699798 / $12.95 | |
| VOL. 63 – CREEDENCE CLEARWATER REVIVAL | 00699802 / $16.99 | |
| VOL. 64 – THE ULTIMATE OZZY OSBOURNE | 00699803 / $16.99 | |
| VOL. 65 – THE DOORS | 00699806 / $16.99 | |
| VOL. 66 – THE ROLLING STONES | 00699807 / $16.95 | |
| VOL. 67 – BLACK SABBATH | 00699808 / $16.99 | |
| VOL. 68 – PINK FLOYD – DARK SIDE OF THE MOON | 00699809 / $16.99 | |
| VOL. 69 – ACOUSTIC FAVORITES | 00699810 / $14.95 | |
| VOL. 70 – OZZY OSBOURNE | 00699805 / $16.99 | |
| VOL. 71 – CHRISTIAN ROCK | 00699824 / $14.95 | |
| VOL. 72 – ACOUSTIC '90S | 00699827 / $14.95 | |
| VOL. 73 – BLUESY ROCK | 00699829 / $16.99 | |
| VOL. 74 – PAUL BALOCHE | 00699831 / $14.95 | |
| VOL. 75 – TOM PETTY | 00699882 / $16.99 | |
| VOL. 76 – COUNTRY HITS | 00699884 / $14.95 | |
| VOL. 77 – BLUEGRASS | 00699910 / $14.99 | |
| VOL. 78 – NIRVANA | 00700132 / $16.99 | |
| VOL. 79 – NEIL YOUNG | 00700133 / $24.99 | |
| VOL. 80 – ACOUSTIC ANTHOLOGY | 00700175 / $19.95 | |
| VOL. 81 – ROCK ANTHOLOGY | 00700176 / $22.99 | |
| VOL. 82 – EASY SONGS | 00700177 / $12.99 | |
| VOL. 83 – THREE CHORD SONGS | 00700178 / $16.99 | |
| VOL. 84 – STEELY DAN | 00700200 / $16.99 | |
| VOL. 85 – THE POLICE | 00700269 / $16.99 | |
| VOL. 86 – BOSTON | 00700465 / $16.99 | |
| VOL. 87 – ACOUSTIC WOMEN | 00700763 / $14.99 | |
| VOL. 88 – GRUNGE | 00700467 / $16.99 | |
| VOL. 90 – CLASSICAL POP | 00700469 / $14.99 | |
| VOL. 91 – BLUES INSTRUMENTALS | 00700505 / $14.99 | |
| VOL. 92 – EARLY ROCK INSTRUMENTALS | 00700506 / $14.99 | |
| VOL. 93 – ROCK INSTRUMENTALS | 00700507 / $16.99 | |
| VOL. 95 – BLUES CLASSICS | 00700509 / $14.99 | |
| VOL. 96 – THIRD DAY | 00700560 / $14.95 | |
| VOL. 97 – ROCK BAND | 00700703 / $14.99 | |
| VOL. 98 – ROCK BAND | 00700704 / $14.95 | |
| VOL. 99 – ZZ TOP | 00700762 / $16.99 | |
| VOL. 100 – B.B. KING | 00700466 / $16.99 | |
| VOL. 101 – SONGS FOR BEGINNERS | 00701917 / $14.99 | |
| VOL. 102 – CLASSIC PUNK | 00700769 / $14.99 | |
| VOL. 103 – SWITCHFOOT | 00700773 / $16.99 | |
| VOL. 104 – DUANE ALLMAN | 00700846 / $16.99 | |
| VOL. 106 – WEEZER | 00700958 / $14.99 | |
| VOL. 107 – CREAM | 00701069 / $16.99 | |
| VOL. 108 – THE WHO | 00701053 / $16.99 | |

| | | |
|---|---|---|
| VOL. 109 – STEVE MILLER | 00701054 / $14.99 | |
| VOL. 111 – JOHN MELLENCAMP | 00701056 / $14.99 | |
| VOL. 112 – QUEEN | 00701052 / $16.99 | |
| VOL. 113 – JIM CROCE | 00701058 / $15.99 | |
| VOL. 114 – BON JOVI | 00701060 / $14.99 | |
| VOL. 115 – JOHNNY CASH | 00701070 / $16.99 | |
| VOL. 116 – THE VENTURES | 00701124 / $14.99 | |
| VOL. 118 – ERIC JOHNSON | 00701353 / $14.99 | |
| VOL. 119 – AC/DC CLASSICS | 00701356 / $17.99 | |
| VOL. 120 – PROGRESSIVE ROCK | 00701457 / $14.99 | |
| VOL. 121 – U2 | 00701508 / $16.99 | |
| VOL. 123 – LENNON & MCCARTNEY ACOUSTIC | 00701614 / $16.99 | |
| VOL. 124 – MODERN WORSHIP | 00701629 / $14.99 | |
| VOL. 125 – JEFF BECK | 00701687 / $16.99 | |
| VOL. 126 – BOB MARLEY | 00701701 / $16.99 | |
| VOL. 127 – 1970S ROCK | 00701739 / $14.99 | |
| VOL. 128 – 1960S ROCK | 00701740 / $14.99 | |
| VOL. 129 – MEGADETH | 00701741 / $16.99 | |
| VOL. 131 – 1990S ROCK | 00701743 / $14.99 | |
| VOL. 132 – COUNTRY ROCK | 00701757 / $15.99 | |
| VOL. 133 – TAYLOR SWIFT | 00701894 / $16.99 | |
| VOL. 134 – AVENGED SEVENFOLD | 00701906 / $16.99 | |
| VOL. 136 – GUITAR THEMES | 00701922 / $14.99 | |
| VOL. 138 – BLUEGRASS CLASSICS | 00701967 / $14.99 | |
| VOL. 139 – GARY MOORE | 00702370 / $16.99 | |
| VOL. 140 – MORE STEVIE RAY VAUGHAN | 00702396 / $17.99 | |
| VOL. 141 – ACOUSTIC HITS | 00702401 / $16.99 | |
| VOL. 142 – KINGS OF LEON | 00702418 / $16.99 | |
| VOL. 144 – DJANGO REINHARDT | 00702531 / $16.99 | |
| VOL. 145 – DEF LEPPARD | 00702532 / $16.99 | |
| VOL. 147 – SIMON & GARFUNKEL | 14041591 / $16.99 | |
| VOL. 149 – AC/DC HITS | 14041593 / $17.99 | |
| VOL. 150 – ZAKK WYLDE | 02501717 / $16.99 | |
| VOL. 153 – RED HOT CHILI PEPPERS | 00702990 / $19.99 | |
| VOL. 157 – FLEETWOOD MAC | 00101382 / $16.99 | |
| VOL. 158 – ULTIMATE CHRISTMAS | 00101889 / $14.99 | |
| VOL. 161 – THE EAGLES – ACOUSTIC | 00102659 / $17.99 | |
| VOL. 162 – THE EAGLES HITS | 00102667 / $17.99 | |
| VOL. 163 – PANTERA | 00103036 / $16.99 | |
| VOL. 166 – MODERN BLUES | 00700764 / $16.99 | |
| VOL. 168 – KISS | 00113421 / $16.99 | |
| VOL. 169 – TAYLOR SWIFT | 00115982 / $16.99 | |
| VOL. 170 – THREE DAYS GRACE | 00117337 / $16.99 | |

**Complete song lists available online.**

*Prices, contents, and availability subject to change without notice.*

HAL•LEONARD® CORPORATION

7777 W. BLUEMOUND RD. P.O. BOX 13819 MILWAUKEE, WI 53213

www.halleonard.com

0713

# Get Better at Guitar

## ...with these Great Guitar Instruction Books from Hal Leonard!

### 101 GUITAR TIPS
*INCLUDES TAB*

STUFF ALL THE PROS KNOW AND USE

*by Adam St. James*

This book contains invaluable guidance on everything from scales and music theory to truss rod adjustments, proper recording studio set-ups, and much more. The book also features snippets of advice from some of the most celebrated guitarists and producers in the music business, including B.B. King, Steve Vai, Joe Satriani, Warren Haynes, Laurence Juber, Pete Anderson, Tom Dowd and others, culled from the author's hundreds of interviews.

00695737 Book/CD Pack.........................$16.95

### AMAZING PHRASING
*INCLUDES TAB*

50 WAYS TO IMPROVE YOUR IMPROVISATIONAL SKILLS

*by Tom Kolb*

This book/CD pack explores all the main components necessary for crafting well-balanced rhythmic and melodic phrases. It also explains how these phrases are put together to form cohesive solos. Many styles are covered – rock, blues, jazz, fusion, country, Latin, funk and more – and all of the concepts are backed up with musical examples. The companion CD contains 89 demos for listening, and most tracks feature full-band backing.

00695583 Book/CD Pack.........................$19.95

### BLUES YOU CAN USE
*INCLUDES TAB*

*by John Ganapes*

A comprehensive source designed to help guitarists develop both lead and rhythm playing. Covers: Texas, Delta, R&B, early rock and roll, gospel, blues/rock and more. Includes: 21 complete solos • chord progressions and riffs • turnarounds • moveable scales and more. CD features leads and full band backing.

00695007 Book/CD Pack.........................$19.95

### FRETBOARD MASTERY
*INCLUDES TAB*

*by Troy Stetina*

Untangle the mysterious regions of the guitar fretboard and unlock your potential. *Fretboard Mastery* familiarizes you with all the shapes you need to know by applying them in real musical examples, thereby reinforcing and reaffirming your newfound knowledge. The result is a much higher level of comprehension and retention.

00695331 Book/CD Pack.........................$19.95

### FRETBOARD ROADMAPS – 2ND EDITION

ESSENTIAL GUITAR PATTERNS THAT ALL THE PROS KNOW AND USE

*by Fred Sokolow*

The updated edition of this bestseller features more songs, updated lessons, and a full audio CD! Learn to play lead and rhythm anywhere on the fretboard, in any key; play a variety of lead guitar styles; play chords and progressions anywhere on the fretboard; expand your chord vocabulary; and learn to think musically – the way the pros do.

00695941 Book/CD Pack.........................$14.95

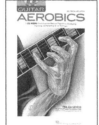

### GUITAR AEROBICS
*INCLUDES TAB*

A 52-WEEK, ONE-LICK-PER-DAY WORKOUT PROGRAM FOR DEVELOPING, IMPROVING & MAINTAINING GUITAR TECHNIQUE

*by Troy Nelson*

From the former editor of *Guitar One* magazine, here is a daily dose of vitamins to keep your chops fine tuned! Musical styles include rock, blues, jazz, metal, country, and funk. Techniques taught include alternate picking, arpeggios, sweep picking, string skipping, legato, string bending, and rhythm guitar. These exercises will increase speed, and improve dexterity and pick- and fret-hand accuracy. The accompanying CD includes all 365 workout licks plus play-along grooves in every style at eight different metronome settings.

00695946 Book/CD Pack.........................$19.99

### GUITAR CLUES
*INCLUDES TAB*

OPERATION PENTATONIC

*by Greg Koch*

Join renowned guitar master Greg Koch as he clues you in to a wide variety of fun and valuable pentatonic scale applications. Whether you're new to improvising or have been doing it for a while, this book/CD pack will provide loads of delicious licks and tricks that you can use right away, from volume swells and chicken pickin' to intervallic and chordal ideas. The CD includes 65 demo and play-along tracks.

00695827 Book/CD Pack.........................$19.95

### INTRODUCTION TO GUITAR TONE & EFFECTS

*by David M. Brewster*

This book/CD pack teaches the basics of guitar tones and effects, with audio examples on CD. Readers will learn about: overdrive, distortion and fuzz • using equalizers • modulation effects • reverb and delay • multi-effect processors • and more.

00695766 Book/CD Pack.........................$14.99

### PICTURE CHORD ENCYCLOPEDIA

This comprehensive guitar chord resource for all playing styles and levels features five voicings of 44 chord qualities for all twelve keys – 2,640 chords in all! For each, there is a clearly illustrated chord frame, as well as *an actual photo* of the chord being played! Includes info on basic fingering principles, open chords and barre chords, partial chords and broken-set forms, and more.

00695224.........................$19.95

### SCALE CHORD RELATIONSHIPS
*INCLUDES TAB*

*by Michael Mueller & Jeff Schroedl*

This book teaches players how to determine which scales to play with which chords, so guitarists will never have to fear chord changes again! This book/CD pack explains how to: recognize keys • analyze chord progressions • use the modes • play over nondiatonic harmony • use harmonic and melodic minor scales • use symmetrical scales such as chromatic, whole-tone and diminished scales • incorporate exotic scales such as Hungarian major and Gypsy minor • and much more!

00695563 Book/CD Pack.........................$14.95

### SPEED MECHANICS FOR LEAD GUITAR
*INCLUDES TAB*

Take your playing to the stratosphere with the most advanced lead book by this proven heavy metal author. *Speed Mechanics* is the ultimate technique book for developing the kind of speed and precision in today's explosive playing styles. Learn the fastest ways to achieve speed and control, secrets to make your practice time really count, and how to open your ears and make your musical ideas more solid and tangible. Packed with over 200 vicious exercises including Troy's scorching version of "Flight of the Bumblebee." Music and examples demonstrated on CD. 89-minute audio.

00699323 Book/CD Pack.........................$19.95

### TOTAL ROCK GUITAR
*INCLUDES TAB*

A COMPLETE GUIDE TO LEARNING ROCK GUITAR

*by Troy Stetina*

This unique and comprehensive source for learning rock guitar is designed to develop both lead and rhythm playing. It covers: getting a tone that rocks • open chords, power chords and barre chords • riffs, scales and licks • string bending, strumming, palm muting, harmonics and alternate picking • all rock styles • and much more. The examples are in standard notation with chord grids and tab, and the CD includes full-band backing for all 22 songs.

00695246 Book/CD Pack.........................$19.99